URBAN
FLOWERS

Creating abundance in a small city garden

For my mother, Sonia Dunster (1936–2016)

URBAN FLOWERS

Creating abundance in a small city garden

Carolyn Dunster   Photography by Jason Ingram

FRANCES
LINCOLN

CONTENTS

MY STORY

For as long as I can remember flowers have played a huge part in my life. I grew up in a small seaside town with the countryside on my doorstep, and from an early age I made a deep and everlasting connection with the natural world, which has fuelled my passion for plants and my career.

My sisters and I would spend hours roaming the fields at the back of our house where I would pluck the wildflowers growing liberally in the hedgerows that criss-crossed the gently rolling landscape. Once home, these brightly coloured gems would be pressed between sheets of weighed-down paper and then transferred to my scrapbook for labelling in my very best handwriting. In those pre-internet days I identified them from a book that had been passed to me from my grandmother: scarlet pimpernel, shepherd's purse, field mouse-ear, bird's-foot trefoil – their enchanting names fired up my girlish imagination and I saw them as characters starring in their very own fairy tales.

Many years later, after I had taken the plunge and decided to make a career out of working with flowers, I realised this game wasn't as whimsical as it sounds. Flowers do indeed have their own special characteristics. On a botanical front, it is how scientists identify them, but speak to anyone in the flower world and they will agree that many blooms have distinctive personality traits. Some are extrovert, gregarious types, brazen even, who love to show off everything they possess. Others are shy and will need a fair amount of coaxing before they agree to display their secret loveliness, but they are somehow all the more beguiling because of their reticence.

Just like shoes and handbags, flowers fall in and out of fashion and the shouty extroverts often fall prey to this, becoming the must-haves for a couple of seasons – yes, darling dahlias, I am looking at you! In the meantime, the more self-effacing types will stay in the background, gradually becoming your lifelong stalwarts. Look no further than the elegant spires of the foxglove family; watch the flowers unfurl to reveal their hidden beauty and you will see what I mean.

Lessons learned

From the study of wildflowers to the cultivation of garden blooms, my upbringing taught me a lot. My childhood home by the sea was built on land sold to a developer by the local farmer, who owned the surrounding fields, and when we moved in we inherited a building site. Through a huge amount of hard, backbreaking work that involved endless digging, we turned the rubble

ABOVE **Me aged five** with my younger sisters in the first flower-filled garden planted by my parents. LEFT **Spiky orange cactus dahlias** steal the show in a mixed planting scheme.

RIGHT **Exploring the fields** beyond our second garden, I discovered my enduring love of the natural world.

BELOW **Wild flowers,** including purple loosestrife and water dropwort, line the riverbanks of the English countryside in late summer. It is permissible to pick invasive species, such as the bright pink Himalayan balsam that you see everywhere, but not rare varieties.

LEFT **My front garden** today is filled with a profusion of lavenders, daisies and roses reminiscent of my childhood.

into a garden full of flowers. Here, in my own dedicated patch, I was allowed to grow what I wanted and my pocket money would go on packets of seeds, much as it does now. Through trial and error I learned what I could easily grow and, more importantly, what gave the most back for its buck.

Moving on

When I left home to pursue my education my parents moved away from the house too. I have never returned to the garden we made but I visit it regularly in my mind. Needless to say, nostalgia dictates that it is always sunny there. I see a picnic spread out on a rug on the lawn, my little white guinea pig is in her run and I am picking a mixed posy of garden blooms to display in my bedroom. The detail is hazy and I can't tell which varieties of flowers I have selected but as I get older I find the overall image comforting. I am guessing that some of the original plants or their offspring are still growing there happily several decades later, demonstrating their power to endure when everything else has changed and the inhabitants have all moved on. I now live

in an inner city borough of one of the largest, busiest metropolises in the world, which could not be more different from the semi-rural bucolic surroundings of my childhood.

I love the city. The constant hustle and bustle, the cosmopolitan mix of people, the fast-moving pace of life and the noise all add up to a vibrancy that makes me feel truly alive and purposeful, but we all need a break from it now and then. I have lived in the same area for many years, moving from a series of rented studios and apartments to a house with a small garden that is now home to my own family. For quite a long time I had no outdoor space and I sought out the parks, public gardens and open green areas as a retreat. I find I need an escape from the constant onslaught of urban living and some green space is essential to me, providing a peaceful sanctuary.

My need to touch and feel and get my hands dirty did not diminish when I came to live in the city. In fact, it's been quite the opposite. My heart has grown even fonder of plants and I have found infinite ways of growing my own flowers, even in the tiniest of spaces – ideas I hope to pass on through the pages of this book.

THE CITY GARDEN

CREATING AN URBAN HABITAT

My aim in this book is to share not only my love of flowers, and the joy they have brought me throughout my life, but also to show how it is possible to grow your own blooms in the heart of an urban area and in the tiniest and most unlikely of spaces.

If you live in a block of flats, a shared house or a property converted from an industrial building you probably won't have a garden, but you may have access to some outside space. Balconies, terraces, rooftops and courtyards are fairly obvious contenders for planting, but I will also look at side returns – those often unloved areas between terraced houses that can be used as more than a place to store your bike. Bin stores, steps, light wells, fire escapes, windowsills, doorways, walls and drainpipes, indeed any exterior part of an urban construction, can be put to service. If you are lucky enough to have a small front or back garden, so much the better, but whatever space you have, plant it rather than paving it over.

Losing ground

We are losing many of our small city gardens, as home owners tarmac or pave them to provide parking spaces and for easy maintenance. The character and environment of city streets changes dramatically when the lawns and flowerbeds are removed and replaced with asphalt, concrete or other hard non-permeable surfaces. We have lost sight of the important contribution that small gardens filled with trees and plants provide, and it is not just that they are

visually more pleasing than a uniform block of hard landscaping. All types of plants clean the air by absorbing pollution, particularly carbon dioxide, and consequently improve its quality. They can mask the constant noise of the city, too, and provide privacy and shelter. In addition, trees and plants form an important part of the armour needed to combat climate change, helping to mitigate the Urban Heat Island effect (UHI) by cooling towns and cities in hot weather and insulating buildings when it's cold, while also providing natural flood defences.

It is estimated that by 2050 eighty per cent of the population in the UK will be living in a town or city, so it is essential that we keep planting our gardens and replacing older trees as they die off to ensure a green legacy for future generations.

TOP LEFT **A plastic bowl** of vermilion bedding plants brightens the grey urban environment.
TOP RIGHT **Vertical planting** against fences and walls creates a welcoming entrance to a period home.
BELOW LEFT **Evergreen topiaries** break up the stark architecture of the city and draw the eye skyward.
ABOVE AND BELOW RIGHT **Beautiful multi-layered** urban planting, designed by Dan Pearson, is full of detail which encourages passers-by to stop and look.

The urban habitat for wildlife

By growing a diverse mix of plants in urban spaces we can protect the environment and maintain delicate ecosystems. The more we grow, the more insects and other wildlife will follow, attracted by the leafy cover and bright flowers. Pollinating insects, especially bees, are essential to our survival, as their job is to transfer pollen from one flower to the stigma of another, enabling seed production and safeguarding the next generation of plants. Without bees many plants, including essential food crops, would die off. Insects of all types also play their part in the food chain and provide a source of nutrition for many birds, which contribute in turn by eating fruit and expelling the undigested seeds that then germinate far away from the parent plants. Look out for plants labelled wildlife friendly and use as many as you can to ensure you are doing your bit.

FAR LEFT **Urban beekeeping** is becoming increasingly popular, and helping to revive a declining bee population. LEFT **Nesting boxes** replicate natural sites in the city, providing shelter and protection for birds that live there. BELOW LEFT AND RIGHT **Insect hotels** offer homes to solitary bees and nectar-rich blooms feed all types of bee.

PLANTING FOR WELL-BEING

Just as plants have a positive effect on birds and insects, they also have a huge impact on us, helping to improve both our physical and mental health. From my own experience I know that they have helped me through the most difficult times in my life.

Nurturing and growing plants is deeply rooted in our DNA. It is what we have done over millennia in order to stay alive. Even if you grow flowers rather than food, the process still reinforces our sense of the world being a magical place. There are aspects of life over which we have no control and I find it nothing short of miraculous that what looks like an unprepossessing speck of dust will germinate given the right conditions. Tucked into a little bed of soil, moistened with a drop of water and left alone in some warmth and light, a single seed will grow into a thing of great beauty. Helping this to happen nourishes the soul.

Learning how to garden teaches us patience and perseverance in a world where we have come to expect instant gratification. In man-made surroundings flowers and plants quench our thirst for natural beauty and through close observation they encourage us to slow down, stop rushing, and to look and look again.

Research is permanently ongoing but it is being proven that 'biophilia', the innate tendency to focus on life and life-like processes, can have positive benefits for human health. Harvard University Professor E.O. Wilson has been researching the effects for many years and has shown that being in nature helps people to

recover from stress and tragedy and is beneficial in the healing process. More importantly, the absence of greenery can actually cause us to feel stressed. Human beings have not totally adapted to living in sterile city surroundings and a lack of access to nature can make us unwell. Through studies in brain science we are learning that surrounding ourselves with flowers and plants positively impacts our psychological well-being.

Seasonal connections

Being outside, connecting with nature, working in the moment to cultivate something for the future, makes us feel better. I certainly need no convincing of this. The more I garden and grow, the more I feel in touch with the seasons, the passing of time, and something intangible that makes me feel literally grounded.

Whether you are in the middle of a busy town or city or in the depths of the countryside, the cyclical repetitiveness of the seasonal changes is calming and reassuring in a world that feels as if it is in constant flux.

Gardening is not only good for the spirit, it also keeps you fit and strong, and there is now a call for it to be available on prescription, as scientific evidence of the benefits increases.

OPPOSITE:
Cut home-grown flowers to decorate your house as well as your garden.
RIGHT: **Growing and nurturing** plants from seed is deeply satisfying and adds to the sum of human contentment. For a tiny investment this tobacco plant rewarded me with flowers that lasted the whole summer.

OPEN THE DOOR TO YOUR COMMUNITY

Try growing a few plants in your front garden or a pot of seasonal flowers on your doorstep and you will be surprised at how these small gestures start up conversations with neighbours, helping to create a sense of community often lost in the city.

If you grow a showstopper on your front step it will probably encourage your neighbours to speak to you – possibly for the first time! It is easy in an urban neighbourhood for everyone to go about their business in such a rush that we neglect the art of a friendly chat. Ironically, in a densely populated street, it is quite possible not to know who lives above your apartment or next door. That used to be my experience. Now that I have a house with a little front garden I find that when I am working in it people walking up and down the road will stop and talk to me. They may initially enquire about a particular flower but quite often that will be the precursor to a completely different conversation.

Through a common interest in gardening I have got to know the lady next door who is in her eighties but still comes outside most days with her trowel in hand. We swap cuttings and give each other tips. I know that what grows well in her garden will grow well in mine and she has many more years of experience than me. Our friendship has taught me that if you need planting advice, ask the owner of the closest, prettiest garden in your street. They will usually be happy to help. As a planting designer, my own garden acts as my shop-window, too, and

I have gained many new clients and expanded my business, as well as making many local friends, through the power of plants.

Working together

Plants help to break down barriers and nowhere more so than in community gardens. If you can only accommodate a few pots, but would like to grow on a larger scale, seek out your local gardening community. Look on your council website for officially organised gardening projects, and offer yourself as a volunteer. If you are a novice, you will learn best by watching more experienced gardeners and these schemes then give you the chance to work under their guidance.

ABOVE: **Rose beds** bring a city street scene to life. CLOCKWISE FROM TOP LEFT **Tree pits** underplanted with seasonal colour bring cheer to urban streets. **A skip garden** created by Global Generation offers young people the chance to gain hands-on horticultural experience. **My own garden** acts as my shop window. **The beautifully tended tree pit,** which I pass every day, brings me great joy as I watch the planting progress. **A pavement garden** allows the locals to grow fruit in a tiny city space. **Community allotments** bring like-minded people together to nurture their crops.

Become a gardening guerilla

Many towns and cities have guerilla gardening groups and initiatives that you can join. These seem to be gaining great mileage in the urban environment and are simply like-minded gardeners who look for ways to green up their local area. For example, in a road close to me the tree pits have been planted with flowers by residents, which has enhanced the streetscape no end and made the walk to the Underground station a lot more pleasant. Elsewhere in my local area, a community pavement garden has been established in a previously dull, bollarded space at the dead-end of a traffic calming scheme. The garden has created a hub for the people who live there to garden and socialise together and provided the children with a safe, green space to play outside.

Greening the city

Whatever its shape or form, you can learn a lot from looking at different types of municipal planting and glean ideas for your own projects. The most inspiring public planting I have come across is at the King's Cross development in central London, masterminded by the property development company Argent LLP. A recently derelict site close to a major railway station, this former industrial area has been transformed under the premise that "life outside buildings is every bit as important as what happens inside them. Water, light and earth combine to create a public realm that is rich in natural green life." In conjunction with a number of landscape architects, award-winning landscape designer Dan Pearson has sensitively planted many of the spaces around the multi-functional buildings, which include smart apartment blocks, offices, social housing, shops, restaurants and schools.

Although the area is in the beating heart of a new, densely occupied urban quarter, which is also the gateway to a huge transport network, there are areas for children to play, and places to sit and relax, where families can congregate and office workers enjoy their lunch.

After 150 years of industrial use, these new public spaces respond to people's needs. The designs reflect the heritage of the site, employing rusty corten steel for the raised beds and oversized planters along the walkways. Filled with grasses and perennials that reflect the natural habitat of a nearby canal corridor and the original plant colonies which established themselves on the old railway lines, they create a sense of wildness. Over 440 species have been planted in the tree-lined avenues, green walls, terraces, roofs and open squares, with lights and water features emphasising the greenery. The planting looks fantastic in every season and can hold its own against the human traffic and air pollution.

CLOCKWISE FROM TOP LEFT:
A pocket park provides a tranquil retreat in the city. **Oversized planters** line the boulevards. **The ethereal beauty** of *Allium stipitatum* 'Mount Everest'. **Raised beds** of rusted corten steel are planted in a naturalistic style, reflecting the wild habitat of the nearby Regent's Canal.

Planting for all

Designed to improve the man-made environment, municipal planting takes many forms and often says a great deal about the upkeep of an area and how well it is cared for. It also encourages civic pride; we are less likely to drop litter in a natural space, for example. We may not even notice public planting a lot of the time – the shrubby greenery in car parks, outside official buildings or in the entrances to doctors' surgeries – but if it wasn't there we would undoubtedly miss it.

Plants soften the hard surfaces and sharp contours of the cityscape. Visually, they make life more pleasant for anyone living and working in high-rise, built-up areas and they improve our daily experience. Plants also break up the building density, giving us a chance to breathe and the opportunity to connect with nature in man-made surroundings. For all the health benefits I have already described it is vital that councils and private developers continue to give weight to the creation of pocket parks, neighbourhood and communal gardens, green squares and the like.

These spaces often include a tried and tested formula of evergreens, used for their year-round colour and ability to retain their shape and structure with the minimum of maintenance, thus keeping costs to a minimum. However, in recent years, some local councils have become more experimental, and these amorphous green shapes are giving way to colourful schemes. Professional designers have been brought in to create mixed and wildflower plantings that help to increase the biodiversity and wildlife population.

I love nothing better than coming across an unexpected urban meadow – the sight immediately takes me back to my childhood. I also use these schemes for inspiration, as they show the range of plants that will cope successfully with pollution and shade, common challenges facing anyone wishing to create a garden in a crowded town or city.

EVALUATING YOUR SPACE

MEASURING & PLANNING YOUR GARDEN

Whatever the size of your outside area, you will be able to grow some plants. Look at the space through fresh gardener's eyes and imagine it filled with flowers, colour, perfume and happiness. The happiness comes not only from the beautiful result, but also from the satisfaction in creating it.

When making a garden, large or small, there will be a certain amount of trial and error. Just accept that you may make the odd mistake as you learn, and enjoy the journey. Whether you have identified a potential new growing space, wish to reshape an existing bed or border, or if you are planning to design a small garden from scratch, the first step is to measure it carefully. This may sound obvious, but it is surprising how many people just make a few rough estimates on the back of an envelope, only to find that their planned planting and features don't fit.

If you have a front or back garden, courtyard, balcony, roof terrace or any area that is bigger than the stretch of your own arm span, enlist some help so that the measurements are accurate. Make a careful note of the length and width of the space, together with the length of the diagonals from corner to corner. Add as many other measurements as possible, including

ABOVE **Make a plan to** help visualise your ideas. LEFT **Custom-made raised beds** can be cut to size and built to fit any space. This one was created from new timber that has weathered beautifully over time and blends perfectly with the cottage-garden style planting in this small garden.

the height of any variations in level, both on the ground if there are steps or terraced areas, and of the boundaries, which may not be the same height on both sides. Once you have the dimensions, plot the area to scale on graph paper.

Adding the details

After creating this plan on paper you will see before you a flat layout of an empty space. Now add in any other relevant information to build up a more detailed image. Include the position of your property and any other buildings, marking the windows and doors that open out on to the area, along with any other access points, such as side doors. Existing beds and borders, retaining walls and fencing should also be drawn in.

The position of pathways, steps, and any structures, such as a greenhouse, shed or covered seating area, need to be indicated on your plan, too, as do shrubs, trees and other plants that you will be keeping. Include at this point any neighbouring trees or shrubs that overhang your space which may affect the light levels and therefore your planting plans.

This plan will help you to build up a visual reference of your space, enabling you to keep a picture in your head of what you hope to achieve.

Design tricks for a small space

Looking at your space from an upstairs window in your own property or your neighbour's can be very helpful in assessing what you have to work with. You will see the garden quite differently if you look down on it and this will help you to unlock potential planting pockets that are not always obvious from the ground.

Different height levels trick the eye into seeing a bigger space, so think about how you can introduce them using the following ideas:

• If the space is completely level, introduce steps that lead down to a central sunken seating area, flowerbed or lawn. The lower garden space does not have to be very deep to achieve the desired effect.
• Install raised beds of different heights.

• Create different planting layers and storeys by using a combination of climbers, small trees, shrubs and herbaceous perennials in a range of heights. Also include evergreen ground-cover plants and fill in any gaps with seasonal flowering bulbs and annuals.
• Grow climbing plants, such as clematis and sweet peas, up obelisks and other frameworks set in the middle of a border.
• Do not restrict taller plants to the back of a border. Tall, thin wispy plants and grasses look good woven through shorter ones.
• Fix shelving to the walls or fences and decorate them with pots of different sizes.
• Install a wooden pergola, small gazebo or an arch to create a new height level that you can clothe with climbers, such as roses.

LEFT **This light well** demonstrates how to make use of different levels. Grow tall flowers in front of your windows so you get the benefit of enjoying them in intricate detail from inside your home.

BELOW **A simple wooden shelf** fixed securely to a fence or wall provides space for displaying a row of pots in similar rustic styles, creating a beautiful vignette in even the tiniest of spaces.

Using the space

Think about how and when you are going to use your garden space. For example, if you are only going to be outside in the evenings you will need to look at lighting and how to install it. This may require an outdoor electrical supply, which will need to be installed by a qualified electrician. If you want to use the garden for entertaining, consider the seating arrangements, or if you plan to make it your personal retreat from the outside world, work out how to optimise your privacy and create a sense of seclusion. In gardens that will be used by small children, you will need to prioritise safety and ensure the space is secure.

The final plan will provide you with a clear outline of what you have to work with and you can then start to fill in the gaps. Play around on paper with new beds, borders and planters of different sizes so there is a good balance of hard and soft landscaping. Allow enough room to accommodate your planting ideas but remember to include somewhere to relax, even if it is just space for some beanbags or folding chairs.

You might try out several different layouts before you find the one that feels right and it can help to go back outside and mark out your plan in three dimensions, using string or chalk to check that everything will fit comfortably. When you are completely happy, you can get out the crayons or felt-tips pens if you are so inclined.

Computer packages

There are various design packages available that allow you to create a garden plan and planting design on the computer, and if you are technically skilled then it is a speedier way of working out how best to use your space.

On the other hand, for me, using a computer removes the fun of designing. I enjoy the creative process and find colouring my planting spaces by hand incredibly therapeutic.

RIGHT **Photograph the space** you want to design and overlay the image with tracing paper to play around with shapes of different sizes that represent your plants.

BELOW **A staggered display** of pots on both sides of these steps creates an instant flexible garden design.

ASSESSING YOUR SITE'S SOIL & ASPECT

Your soil type and the way your garden faces, as well as the amount of sunlight it receives, are the most important factors to consider when planning a planting scheme, and they will determine the long-term success of the plants you choose to grow.

Checking the soil

Soil sustains plants. Together with warmth, light and water, it provides an anchor and food source, which plants depend on for healthy growth. If you are planning a redesign of existing beds or borders you have inherited, or if you simply want to embellish the planting, then look at what is already flourishing. Identify the plants that are growing well, and then check what kind of soil they thrive in, which will indicate the type you have in your garden. You can also work it out by looking at and handling your soil (above).

Clay tends to be reddish in colour. It is also sticky when wet, has a smooth texture, and will keep its shape when rolled into a ball. Clay soils are prone to waterlogging and are difficult to dig, forming a hard pan on the surface when dry. However, they tend to be rich in nutrients.

Sand can be identified by its gritty texture and it will sift through your fingers. When damp, sandy soils will fall apart if you try to roll them into a ball. Easy to dig, they are also prone to drought and tend to hold few plant nutrients.

Silt has a silky or soapy texture when wet, and has similar characteristics to sand, although it contains more nutrients. Silty soils are also prone to compacting, but retain water well, which plants can take up easily.

Moist loam is the soil most gardeners dream about. It contains an almost equal mix of sand and clay particles and holds plant nutrients and water well, while also allowing free drainage, providing ideal growing conditions. You can help to achieve this optimum mix, whatever your soil type, by digging in well-rotted organic matter, such as garden compost, or spreading it over the surface as a mulch for the worms to take down into the soil.

Soil-based and multi-purpose composts are made from either a mix of soil and decayed organic matter, or just organic matter, which may include peat. They provide the best growing media for pot-grown flowers, and you can buy them in plastic sacks from your local garden centre or DIY store, or order them online for a home delivery.

Monitoring light levels

Assessing the aspect of your garden means working out which direction it faces and its exposure to sunlight. A compass will tell you this, but you can observe for yourself by noting where the sun rises and sets.

Buying potting compost

If you don't have much storage space in your garden then buy small bags of compost to use as you need them. One huge sack may be more economical but if you have nowhere to keep it, this is a problem in itself. There is nothing more unattractive than a half-opened bag spilling out its contents among a beautiful display of plants.

I am often asked if it is possible to reuse potting compost after a season's flowers have finished, and the answer is yes – if you replace the goodness. You can incorporate fresh nutrients by adding 'blood fish and bone', a granular fertiliser which is not as grisly as it sounds. After removing the debris from any previous planting, combine it with the old compost, following the dosage recommendations on the pack. Wear gardening gloves and prepare for the pungent smell – it is no worse than the odour of a farmyard but something that as city dwellers we are not accustomed to.

South facing: sun all day from sunrise to sunset.
East facing: sun in the morning.
West facing: sun in the afternoon and evening.
North facing: little direct sunlight (but don't let that put you off – you can still grow flowers).

Typical city gardens and courtyards are bordered on every side by mature gardens, high walls and fences. Tall neighbouring tree canopies and buildings will reduce light levels but they also create a mild microclimate. Wind, rain and snow can damage plants and freezing temperatures will kill tender or half-hardy types, but if your space is protected from the elements they have a much greater chance of surviving. The same applies to balconies and terraces sheltered by the walls of a property. Unless they face north, they will form sun traps that provide an opportunity to grow a range of Mediterranean plants, which thrive in these conditions.

If wind is a problem on a roof terrace, try creating a barrier or windbreak with a row of tall flexible plants like bamboo to mitigate the effects. Or use shelving units or purpose-made

ABOVE **This south-facing terrace** is in direct sunlight all day long and provides a home for pots of geraniums (*Pelargonium*) and Mediterranean herbs that love hot, dry conditions and thrive with minimal watering.

Tips to lighten cold, dark spaces

- Strategically placed mirrors will reflect light into a small dark space and make it appear bigger.
- Install lighting from an outdoor electrical point or string up battery-operated or solar-powered overhead fairy lights, which can be woven through shrubs.
- Hang up hurricane lamps from hooks on walls or install shelving to display them.
- Make a trail of tea lights in small glass tumblers or empty glass jam jars to lighten up the ground.
- Invest in a portable outdoor fire pit – there are many available for small gardens – to create a sense of warmth in chilly spaces and to encourage you to spend more time outside.

A small fire pit introduces a little extra warmth.

plant stands to provide added protection for smaller plants in containers and pots.

North-facing gardens, dark side returns or dingy basement light wells present challenges for the flower gardener, but even these can be transformed with a few design tricks. Painting boundaries a pale colour will help, and using Perspex or reinforced glass instead of tiles on the roof of a side return will also increase light levels.

Planting in gloomy spaces

Many plants love shade or dappled light. Look for large-leaved foliage plants, including hostas, ferns and calla lilies. White or pale-coloured blooms, such as *Vinca minor* f. *alba*, will also shine in dark spaces. Some climbers prefer shade too. The climbing hydrangea, *Hydrangea anomala* subsp. *petiolaris* is a case in point, and will cover a gloomy wall with lacy white florets in summer. Another good choice is the variegated ivy *Hedera helix* 'Glacier', or try the climbing roses 'Albéric Barbier', 'Madame Alfred Carrière' and 'New Dawn', which all grow happily in part shade, covering walls with their scented blooms.

ABOVE RIGHT **The walls of this dark courtyard** garden are clothed with white-flowered climbing hydrangeas (*Hydrangea anomala* subsp. *petiolaris*) that instantly make the space feel lighter and less oppressive.
OPPOSITE **Dappled light** provides the perfect conditions for a wide range of plants. Look for those that show a preference for partial shade, such as box (*Buxus*) and hardy geraniums, if your space does not face due south.

MAINTAINING YOUR GARDEN

No planted space will magically look after itself, and even the tiniest of containers requires watering and a little vigilance to keep the plants happy and healthy. Before you embark on any gardening project it's essential to be realistic about the time you have to devote to its care.

Choosing a watering system

You only need to water established plants in the ground when the weather has been dry for a week or two, so in a tiny space wandering around with a watering can in high summer should not be too demanding. However, if you have plants in pots, you will need to water them regularly from spring to autumn, regardless of the weather, as their leaves can shield the compost, leaving it dry even after a deluge.

In a larger space, it makes sense to invest in a hose so that watering does not become a chore. If a daily commitment to watering is too much, consider installing an irrigation system. You can buy various kits and there are also apps available that enable you to water via a smartphone. If you are gardening on a terrace or balcony where there is no outside tap and you have to go up and down stairs to fetch water, think about installing a water butt, bucket or rain harvesting system to provide a more readily available supply.

Tidying, weeding and pruning

Borders, raised beds and containers need to be maintained to look their best. Pottering about with a pair of secateurs and a trowel should be a calming, relaxing activity and if you can set aside some time each week for deadheading, tidying and cutting back, you will stay on top of it. You will gradually learn the difference between a cultivated flower and a weed, and the latter will only grow where there is space, so keep bare soil to a minimum. Use ground-cover plants to keep weeds at bay and, after planting beds and pots, dress the surface with stone chippings, gravel or bark to suppress them and make it easier to remove any that do sneak in.

LEFT **Rain-water harvesting** systems like this one provide easy access to water where no outside tap is available. RIGHT **Plants in pots** and containers will require watering daily, or even twice a day, in the summer.

USING POTS & CONTAINERS

All the step-by-step projects in this book are ideas for growing flowers in containers, because for many people this is their only option. Pots provide flexibility and the chance to grow all kinds of plants, creating a beautiful floriferous space where there is no soil or alternative area for planting.

One large container provides the means to create a miniature garden, while several offer the opportunity to produce a series of little plots, with different types of flowers in each that collectively complement one another. If you are using a range of containers of varying sizes and heights, made from different materials and with different finishes, then play around with them before planting to get the presentation right. Small or shallow pots may be best displayed on wooden or metal boxes or tables and chairs so they can be seen – they will get lost if set on the ground. Some of the best effects can be created by grouping small miscellaneous pots in uneven numbers and introducing some repetition in the planting. Alternatively, you can use a few containers of the same style, perhaps in different sizes, to help your design flow.

The Japanese style of gardening, where bonsai trees and other miniature evergreens are cultivated in pots, demonstrates how every detail matters in an intimate space. Each individual plant is carefully pruned and shaped to create an overall environment that feels tranquil and serene, where nothing jars or clashes. In the same way, container gardening allows you the luxury of tending to your flowers and paying particular attention to each one, so that you come to recognise its various habits.

If your time is limited, invest in just one large or medium-sized container, which will be easier to care for than a series of smaller pots. Try planting it with evergreens or grasses to create a permanent backdrop, and use the rest of the space to experiment with seasonal blooms that introduce splashes of colour, but can be easily removed when they have finished flowering.

Setting the stage for flowers

Stairs and steps offer fantastic planting and staging opportunities. Pots and planters can be displayed on them at different levels, and you can move things around to show them off when they are at their best and then hide or remove them when they start to go over. Growing some herbs or scented shrubs that release their perfume as you brush past provides a lovely way to make use of this type of space. If you have to access your planting area via stairs or steps,

ABOVE **Houseleeks** require almost no watering.
LEFT **Selecting a tonal colour scheme**, such as blue–purple, for a range of different plants in a single container is pleasing on the eye.

Portable plastic trugs make lightweight, durable and inexpensive planters for summer bedding plants.

to get to a roof terrace, for example, bear in mind the logistics of going up and down with your arms full. Use lightweight containers that are not easily broken, or consider small growbags with handles or portable plastic tubs. Buy compost in small bags that are easy to carry, and fill all your pots, tubs and bags when they are in situ.

Keep up the suspension

Container planting need not be restricted to pots that are set on the ground. There are many planters designed for specific situations, or you can fashion your own from existing pots with the addition of sturdy hooks and wires. Window boxes and balcony planters can be fastened onto railings and you can create a hanging garden in pots suspended from hooks on window and door frames to make a planting space out of thin air. With a little imagination you can create a container garden almost anywhere.

Watering tips for containers

- Pots dry out quickly, which is the main reason why plants in containers fail to thrive. Water daily or twice daily in the summer if it is hot and dry.
- Water directly onto the compost, rather than on the foliage or flowers, so the roots of the plant get wet.
- Use sphagnum moss to cover the compost. It retains water and will stop it drying out.
- Experiment with water-retaining crystals and gels but never dispose of them down a sink or drain as they will block it.
- If a pot has completely dried out and the plant is wilted, stand it in a large bucket of cold water for 24 hours to revive it.
- Use drip trays, pot bases and saucers to collect water when it rains; they also prevent dirty water that has drained out of a planted pot from staining flooring.
- If you are going away, or are unable to water on a daily basis, make your own drip bottles. You can buy kits with fitted adaptors (*see below*) with porous ceramic cones that you screw onto plastic or glass bottles of any size. Fill the bottles with water and insert them in your pots to keep the compost and plants' roots moist.

ABOVE LEFT **Aged terracotta pots** and zinc buckets look lovely filled with herbs and trailing ivy. ABOVE RIGHT **Pot up vintage vases** but be sure to incorporate extra drainage material such as grit or gravel below the compost. BELOW RIGHT **Upcycled cans** make cheap, pretty alternatives to traditional pots; just make drainage holes in the bases. BELOW LEFT **A galvanised dustbin** will provide a home for a small tree or large shrub like this skimmia.

WALLS, ROOFS & OTHER FLAT SURFACES

Walls and boundary surfaces form the backbone of urban topography, but rather than hemming us in, they can be embraced to form an integral part of the garden, with plants growing up, through and over them. Try these ideas for greening up your boundaries and buildings.

Walled, private gardens have always been seen as desirable spaces, but many of the large town houses that featured them have been divided up into smaller apartments, maisonettes and duplexes, and their gardens have been carved up too. But more recently, I have visited a number of properties where the owners have reversed this trend. They have knocked down dividing walls and removed fences to create large communal gardens where there is space for everyone to enjoy being outside and those that want to get their hands dirty can really get stuck in.

While you may not be in a position to remove a wall, remember that it does not need to be a physical or psychological barrier. If your neighbours have beautiful gardens, there is no need to block them out. Use them as inspiration and borrow their backdrop, if it is attractive, and integrate it into your own design. Match the planting on either side of a wall and it will be doubly lush and generous. I have planted a fig adjacent to where my neighbour has one, so that in the height of summer it looks like one enormous tree, and we share the fruit too.

Try integrating your walls or fences using the tips opposite, so that they form as much a part of the garden as the planting and other hard

landscaping features. Blurring the boundaries in this way will help to make your space feel bigger and less restricted.

Green roofs and other flat spaces

Any flat roof can provide a fantastic planting opportunity but before you start such a project check the rules and regulations pertaining to usage, as well as health and safety requirements. For many projects, other than plants in pots or containers, this will mean bringing in professional help. For the purposes of growing flowers to pretty up an ugly flat roof or to make use of the only space available, whether it is a bin or log store, communal bike shelter or garden shed, you will not need permission if you own the freehold. In other cases, check with your landlord or management company.

Pre-grown sedum matting, which is widely available on easy-to-lay rolls, requires very little maintenance and no watering. Sedums will provide you with a year-round green roof but if you want more seasonal colour, then wildflower turf in a roof meadow mix is the answer. Turf is denser and heavier than sedum matting, so you will need to check the load capacity of your roof first. It also rolls out like carpet, and is grown on a netting base that will eventually biodegrade. Meadow turf attracts insects and birds and will bring colour and character to an uninviting flat space.

You can also plant the roofs of bin or log stores, insect hotels (opposite), sheds and storage units in shallow crates tailored to fit them; fill these with lightweight compost and drought-tolerant plants.

RIGHT **A green roof** made up of drought-tolerant houseleeks (*Sempervivum*) and sedums will transform a plain wooden shed into a beautiful garden feature.

Tips for integrating walls into your design

- Use the top of a low wall to display a row of pots.
- When planting in the ground, only use drought-tolerant species directly next to a wall and avoid disturbing the foundations – if you hit brick or concrete move your hole further away. Plant other species about 20cm (8in) from a wall or fence.
- Add compost and fertiliser when planting as the soil close to walls is always dry and low in nutrients.
- Make the most of the protection, shelter and extra warmth. A wall retains heat so use it as the backdrop for a bed of sun-loving annual cutting flowers.
- Grow tall, leggy, annual plants that would normally require staking against a wall with wires fixed to it, so you can tie on the stems more discreetly.
- Use proprietary wall planting pockets to create a green wall with small flowers and foliage plants (left).

NOOKS, CRANNIES & DIFFICULT CORNERS

Every space contains one or more difficult corners. At worst they are dark, neglected spaces with no signs of life or vegetation, but pay them a little attention, and they can be transformed into extra growing spaces with the help of some tough, accommodating plants.

ABOVE **Ferns and ivies** lighten up dark, shady corners. TOP RIGHT **Leave planting pockets** along the edges of steps and raised beds, and break up paved areas with drought-loving plants to soften the hard landscaping. BOTTOM RIGHT **A log pile** is easy to assemble and creates a natural habitat for wildlife and plants.

Clumps of the little daisy, *Erigeron karvinskianus* (pictured above), will quickly take up residence in cracks between bricks or timber joists and these joyful little flowers, which bloom virtually all year round in the city, will bring cheer to any nook. Another plant to encourage is *Campanula poscharskyana*. It grows anywhere and everywhere and will form small mounds of bell-shaped purple or white flowers in the most unlikely spots. Either can be planted directly into a crack in a wall by gently inserting the roots of a young plant into some dampened compost and securing it in place with moss (*see opposite*).

Greening up hard surfaces

In hard paved spaces, which may on first sight appear totally uninhabitable, try installing a small log pile to create a natural setting. The logs will gradually attract lichens and mosses and become a haven for insects and other wildlife. It is also possible to use hard surfaces to create tiny planting spaces. A few large boulders, pebbles and gravel surrounding a series of pots will provide a welcoming environment for colonising plants to take root. By creating these artificial pockets you can transform the most inhospitable spot into a plant-friendly place.

Planting into a wall

If the little gaps and cracks you want to plant up are devoid of any soil then fill them first. This is easy to do if you wet some soil or potting compost – a clay-based soil is perfect for this as it will stay in place more easily – and push it into the gaps. You may need to scrape away some of the existing mortar with a small knife to increase the size of the crack before wrapping the roots of a tiny plant or seedling in damp soil and gently inserting it. If the plant feels too loose or insecure, use some moss or other organic matter, such as wet leaves, to push in around the roots to keep them in place. Remember to keep watering your plants gently until the roots take hold. Spraying with a mister is the best option as this won't dislodge the plants. Good planting choices for cracks in walls include the trailing bellflower, *Campanula poscharskyana*, *Erigeron karvinskianus*, *Vinca minor* (periwinkle), *Galium odoratum* (sweet woodruff), creeping thymes, and small-leaved ivies.

Campanula poscharskyana, or trailing bellflower, will take root easily in a crack in an old wall, its leafy stems and flowers soon covering the bricks.

INTRODUCING PRIVACY

In a densely populated area living cheek by jowl with other people is the quid pro quo. Although seclusion has to be a state of mind rather than a reality, since it is impossible to create total privacy in most urban gardens, some design tricks can help.

Most urban gardens are overlooked from every angle by neighbouring buildings, and if you live in a flat or an apartment with a garden, then your space will be on view to the people living above you as well. Even if you are lucky enough to have a small area that isn't totally overlooked you will still be aware of the noise and activity of other people going about their daily lives.

Accepting your lack of privacy is half the battle, but you can still design a quiet, tranquil space for yourself. A sense of privacy is all that is required. This can be achieved by using plants as a screening device or by installing fencing or trellis to create the impression of being in a self-contained private space. Horizontal fencing panels work really well along boundaries because they are not solid and allow light to filter through. They look attractive when bare but also provide a good support for climbing plants to scramble up.

Making a peaceful haven

Creating a false boundary in front of your existing walls and fences offers an added feeling of protection. It may mean losing some space but this can be worth it if seclusion is your top priority. By installing trellis in front of an existing fence or wall you also double the planting opportunities, but make sure that the original boundary is clothed in an evergreen that requires little maintenance if the area is difficult to access.

Make use of existing tree canopies, and don't cut back everything in sight, as this will expose your space. Where the branches from a neighbour's tree overhang your garden but also block out their windows, leave them in place and prune judiciously. Any tree, however small, provides shelter and security, so if you have space, I would advise planting one – see pp. 74-75 for planting suggestions. Olive trees or large shrubs in pots on balconies and terraces can be positioned to obscure overlooking windows. Bamboos make particularly effective screening and their rustling leaves can muffle other intrusive noises too. Bubbling water in a small bowl or fountain will have the same effect.

Positioning seats and chairs so that you have your back to the boundary will focus your attention into, rather than out of, your garden, and increase the sense of privacy and protection. Also install a pergola or other structure over your seating area and clothe it with climbers, such as scented roses and jasmine, to mask prying eyes and help establish your own personal Eden in the midst of the urban frenzy.

ABOVE LEFT **Painted horizontal** fencing panels make an attractive enclosure. ABOVE RIGHT **A small pergola** creates a private seating area. BELOW RIGHT **Multi-stemmed birch** trees prevent passers-by from looking in but don't block the light. BELOW LEFT **Trellis** covered in foliage works as a second boundary to create an added sense of privacy. OPPOSITE **Place seats** to face into the garden, with their backs to the boundary.

CHOOSING A STYLE

PERSONALISING YOUR SPACE

Painting walls, adding pots and selecting garden furniture that suits your style combine to create a space that feels like home. When deciding on a look for your schemes outside, start by taking a close look at your interior décor and reflecting those images beyond your back door.

Do you live in a space of clean, sharp lines and uncluttered minimalism, or perhaps you prefer a shabby chic look put together with a mix of vintage items that show the patina of age? What do your soft furnishings say about your preferred choice of pattern, colour and texture? Think about these style factors to help clarify what you find visually pleasing and for some pointers on how to proceed outdoors.

Ideally, there should be a seamless flow between inside and out: a well-executed garden improves the view from indoors (pictured above) and vice-versa. You are effectively creating an extension of your home, while also making a green sanctuary where you can retreat from the hustle and bustle of daily life. The furniture and soft furnishings, pots and accessories you choose are the props that will help you to set the scene.

When transforming a small outdoor space, try painting the surfaces, furniture and pots the same colour to create a uniform look that pulls everything together. Use exterior eggshell, gloss or garden stains, which help to protect wood

LEFT **Make a small space** your own with natural finds and add seasonal plants in little pots grouped together on a metal table to create a temporary still life.

or prevent metal from rusting too. Also look to nature for inspiration. Cloudy blues and off-whites reflect the sky, or try sharp fresh lemon-limes that echo young spring foliage or the subtle grey-greens of mosses and lichens. Damson shades mirror autumn fruits and berries, and the stony, mottled hues of a pile of pebbles and tawny tones of bark and stems provide more colour solutions. Identify which shades will provide the right foil for you so you can decorate a space that echoes the natural world, where you will feel comfortable and secure.

If your planting area is communal or you live in rented accommodation, with no means to personalise your space, then simply paint a series of containers or window boxes in a colour that you like to create your own personal stamp. Or consider making a portable backdrop with waterproofed fabric rather than paint, which you can take with you when you move.

Sourcing props

To accommodate flowering plants in a tiny space it is not necessary to go out and spend a lot of money on pots and accessories. It's amazing what you can use with a bit of imagination, a lick of paint and a glue gun. Have a good look around the rooms of your home to see if you already have some containers that would work as planters. Storage boxes, suitcases and trunks, kitchen paraphernalia such as mixing bowls, saucepans or cake tins, empty food cans, and redundant dining china can all be recycled and used as receptacles for your plants. You can plant into almost any kind of container providing you incorporate some means of drainage to prevent waterlogging. This either means drilling or using a nail and hammer to create drainage holes in the bottom of wooden, metal or plastic containers, or adding some small stones, horticultural grit or broken crocks to repurposed china. Kitchen colanders are the perfect planting vessels, given that they have ready-made drainage holes. A mini colander in a bright colour

can be planted with a single trailing plant for a quick five-minute project that brings instant joy. Add either macramé or plaited plastic twine before planting and suspend it from a bracket.

From the old to the new

Salvage yards, garage and car boot sales, junk shops and hardware stores often throw up inexpensive finds that can be repurposed for outdoor use. Small wooden pallets that are often available free of charge from garden centres or DIY shops can be dismantled, sanded, reassembled and painted to make shelving, wall planters or trays for seeds. Wooden fruit crates and old wine boxes also fit the bill.

You can customise ugly plastic plant pots by covering them with dried leaves, moss and bark, or use magazine tearsheets to create papier mâché cachepots – a coat of varnish will make them waterproof. Or disguise a large plastic pot with a length of hessian – wrap it like a present and secure with rope. I also use rice or coffee bean sacks in a similar way; you can buy these online. Empty cooking oil drums and catering size tins from fast food outlets can be planted up too, while shopping bags and woven plastic or jute baskets can hide small and medium-sized pots of flowers. Place them inside and cover the compost with sphagnum moss or bark chippings, so that your flowers look as if they are growing in their own self-contained garden.

If you are intending to purchase new props, containers and furniture, look online or visit high street stores or your local garden centre to research the ranges on offer. The choice is endless, so have a clear idea of what you are looking for and stick to it.

LEFT **A hard-wearing woven bag** made from recycled plastic makes an excellent portable container. Just pop your potted plants inside and cover the top with moss.

CLOCKWISE FROM TOP LEFT
Use a fruit crate fixed to a fence or wall to display flowers and artefacts. **Three pots** of different sizes but the same colour are stacked up to make a tiered display. **Create a pretty backdrop** with a floral collage behind a wire mesh shelving unit. **A bright plastic kitchen colander** has ready-made drainage holes for trailing petunias. *Campanula poscharskyana* spills out of a vintage suitcase.

DEFINING YOUR STYLE

The architectural vernacular of your property will largely dictate the details of your outdoor space, while the city skyline, dominated by tower blocks and punctuated with construction machinery, will inevitably impose itself on your personal space as well.

We cannot borrow from a city landscape as we would in the countryside to create bucolic, far-reaching vistas. Instead, we have to translate and disseminate dreams of a rural idyll and interpret them to create a sense of being at one with nature in our small urban spaces. I have defined three different styles on the following pages that will hopefully allow you to do this.

It is important to note, however, that there are no hard and fast rules, particularly when it comes to plants. It is the way you stage your planting that will dictate your style, rather than the plants themselves. A sense of personal style comes from having confidence in your taste, so pick what you like from my ideas and adapt them to work in your own space.

To source ideas, browse through Instagram and Pinterest, look at magazines, collect wallpaper and fabric samples with patterns of foliage and flowers that jump out at you, and pick up natural finds such as leaves with shapes

or textures that appeal to you. Assemble all your chosen images and objects to create a mood board, which will allow you to see how they can come together as a whole. This will also give you a clear sense of direction to follow and allow you to develop your own garden style.

ABOVE **Clipped box balls** set the scene for a classic garden style in front of a period London house.
RIGHT **A colour-themed mood board** of images and natural finds creates a visual guide and allows you to play around with ideas before committing to purchases.

RURBAN STYLE

For city dwellers who dream
of gardening in a rural location.

CLASSIC STYLE

Imports traditional elements of
a country estate into a city garden.

CONTEMPORARY STYLE

Embraces all that is new
in modern urban gardening.

RURBAN STYLE

The melding of cottage planting and rustic props, this style brings together key elements from country gardens. And while there may not be space for roses to ramble around the front door, it is easy to distill many features into a small urban space.

Traditionally, the gardens of country cottages are cultivated to be sustainable and productive. Flowers, fruits and vegetables jostle for space in the same bed, and gardeners grow in abundance what they like to cook and eat. The brightly coloured flowers found in these gardens tend to be annuals grown for picking and displaying on the kitchen table, giving to neighbours, or selling as surplus bunches at the garden gate. With space often at a premium, vegetables and flowers are planted in neat orderly rows that can be easily reached for harvesting.

Colourful abundance

At the beginning of the season, cottage gardeners often plant up a small raised bed or defined rectangular patch following a strong linear form. There may be a row of lettuces set out next to a row of beans climbing up wigwam frames; or chard, with its dazzling line-up of rainbow stems, interspersed with vibrant orange pot marigolds (*Calendula officinalis*) that help to ward off unwanted predators, such as aphids, while also providing food for bees. Neatly clipped mounds of rosemary, thyme and lavender are used to create a textural border enclosing all this bounty. By midsummer the cottage garden

is ablaze with colour and full to bursting with an array of edible produce for the kitchen, to be eaten straight away, bottled and pickled, or turned into jam, conserves or syrups.

Adapting a cottage style

While we do not necessarily need to garden in this way for self-sufficiency in the city, cottage style is appealing to many and simple to adapt. Visiting urban allotments will provide plenty of inspiration and ideas. Also look for flowering plants that are closely related to vegetables, such as the cardoon (*Cynara cardunculus*), a member of the artichoke family, with its large silvery spiny leaves on strong stems that support huge purple thistles in high summer. I plant big cabbages in pots on either side of my front door too – not for eating but for their shape and texture. Other brassicas, such as kale, can also be grown specifically for their looks and striking colours.

Alliums, or ornamental onions, are a cottage garden stalwart which hold their own in the city, with their dramatic purple or white spherical heads, some the size of tennis balls. These pack a punch in a small space and can be grown in containers from bulbs planted in the autumn (*see pp.88-89*). If space is very limited try growing

OPPOSITE **Metal planters** filled with cosmos suit a rurban plot. RIGHT **The small space** in front of this shed allows for a seating area, pots planted with *Agapanthus* and herbs, as well as a climber clinging to the sides on a trellis frame. The rustic materials and choice of plants provide a perfect example of rurban style.

chives instead; their flowers achieve the same effect on a smaller scale. Experiment with other flowering herbs, too, such as chicory, borage and sweet woodruff.

To pretty things up, include the frillier varieties of hollyhocks and a few delphiniums, which will introduce some height and stand tall and upright, while also providing great blooms for cutting. And no cottage garden would be complete without nasturtiums. Among the easiest flowers to grow from seed, both in pots and in the ground (*see project on pp.132-133*), the leaves and flowers are edible, imparting a peppery flavour that will enliven any green salad. Try 'Black Velvet' for a sedate dark hue or jazz things up with the bright orange and yellow 'Tom Thumb'. Sow them alongside cut-and-come-again lettuces or rocket in a window box or crate on your doorstep, and pick as required.

ABOVE **This naturalistic planting** includes cottage garden favourites, such as alliums and aquilegias. OPPOSITE, CLOCKWISE FROM TOP LEFT **Use plant supports** in a rusty finish to complement your schemes. **Scour salvage yards** and antique fairs for garden furniture. **Mix up small planting** schemes with wildflowers and grasses grown from seed. **Customise cheap plastic** pots by covering them with tree bark or varnished papier mâché. **Fill a raised bed** with seasonal flowers, such as sweet peas and scarlet monarda.

Mixing things up

The rustic element of rurban-styled gardens lies in the props and containers you select. Grow as much as possible in a variety of different-sized pots and containers, where the plants rather

than the pots take centre stage. You are aiming for an effortless, artisan look, where everything appears to have been put together by accident, but there is an art to achieving this in a small space without it appearing messy. Firstly, discard anything that is too uniform, new or shiny. Old, hand-thrown terracotta pots in a variety of sizes always look attractive, but if necessary buy new ones, paint them with organic natural yoghurt and leave outside to weather. They will gradually go green and mossy over time. My preferred shape is a tall long tom, which is deep enough to grow delphiniums and hollyhocks without having to stake them. A row of these containers on an urban terrace will immediately summon up the cottage garden aesthetic.

Boxed-in displays

Vintage wooden boxes and crates come into their own in rurban-styled gardens. You can find them online or at city flower markets. Alternatively, your local greengrocer will have flimsier versions made of plywood, which can be painted and varnished for planting up outside. The sturdier crates can also be used to make impromptu shelving for pots and containers, if you have space to fix them along your boundaries.

The odd chamber pot, ceramic butler's sink or glazed clay pot will also look pretty set among wooden crates and filled with herbs or trailing annuals. Use natural jute twine to tie in any tall plants, and include wooden-handled tools, trugs and baskets, cane or rattan furniture and distressed tables and chairs to complete the look.

OPPOSITE **Wrap a large plastic pot** in a coffee or rice sack to show off cottage-style plants in a rustic setting.
ABOVE LEFT **A stack of hessian sacks** used as growing bags make good planters for edible flowers, such as nasturtiums and pot marigolds (*Calendula*).
ABOVE RIGHT **Line a wooden crate** with hessian before planting to prevent any soil from falling away. Use plants with shallow rooting systems that quickly form a carpet to cover the surface, such as this saxifrage.

CLASSIC STYLE

Classic style never dates. Imparting the elegance and craftsmanship of a bygone era, recreate the look in an urban outdoor setting by researching the design elements of grand period country houses and gardens, and include features that will work on a reduced scale in your city space.

Visiting heritage properties will give you some classical design ideas, which you can then interpret to suit your space and purse. The huge estates of these magnificent houses are often divided into small garden rooms to make them more accessible and to reduce their vast scale. Here, formality, symmetry and the use of correct proportion together impose an overall sense of order. Using pots or planters of the same size and shape, and spacing them equally around a central focal point, such as a fountain, statue or a circular raised bed, will create a similar effect.

Classical proportions

A perfect way of working out the measurements for the design of a small classically styled space is to follow the rules of the golden ratio. Also known as the golden mean, the golden section

ABOVE **The rosette leaf pattern** of the *Aloe polyphylla* plant is an example of the golden spiral. It is a naturally perfect shape that is closely aligned to the golden ratio, which is used a design tool in classic styles.
LEFT **A reproduction stone urn** immediately sets the scene for classic styling in a small city garden. Filled with *Cosmos atrosanguineus* 'Chocamocha', the dark red flowers smell quite addictively of chocolate.

and the golden spiral it is the formula that defines beauty and has been in practice for millennia. It works using a ratio of 1:1.618 and provides designers with the golden rectangle, allowing them to achieve perfectly balanced measurements to work out spatial dimensions, such as parterres, that subconsciously please the eye. Use the ratio as a guide to lay out a small rectangular plot by drawing a square on the ground with chalk. Then use a piece of rope to form a line from the midpoint of one side of the square to an opposite corner. Secure the rope at the midpoint and use it to draw an arc, which will provide the top line of the rectangle, thereby achieving the correct aesthetic proportions.

You can also see the golden ratio employed in art and architecture, but it takes its roots in the natural world. Look at flowers and seedheads and you will see that the petals or pods are in exact proportion to each other in length and diameter; the spiral patterns on pine cones and shells are other examples of nature's perfection.

Elegant additions

Keeping spacing at the forefront of your mind, consider proportion and shapes while looking for props and furnishings. Source traditional

Versailles-styled planters in wood, lead, copper or verdigris. Ideally, purchase two or four in identical or decreasing sizes so you can place them symmetrically. A pair of cast iron or stone urns planted with box balls and set on either side of a doorway looks welcoming and elegant. New

ABOVE **Parterre gardens** demonstrate the symmetrical ground plan and orderly planting of the classical style. OPPOSITE, CLOCKWISE FROM TOP LEFT **Climbing roses** inject a sense of romance to classic formal garden style. **Black planters** that echo the colour and style of the front door provide a smart welcome to this elegant home. **Hurricane lanterns**, white paintwork and pots of arum lilies bring a touch of sophistication to a small urban space. *Hydrangea macrophylla* makes a strong statement against a clipped yew hedge. **The colourful planting** in these traditional window boxes is changed regularly with the seasons.

stoneware or fibre clay reproductions work just as well. You can also find old stone birdbaths, water basins and other vintage garden items in junk shops and salvage yards. They may be chipped or cracked but can be repaired with quick-dry cement filler, which will be disguised once they are filled with compost and plants. If covered with lichens and moss, rub them gently with a wire brush, but do not try to clean them so that they are immaculate – their age and history is very much part of their appeal.

Traditional glasshouses, orangeries and conservatories offer great styling inspiration too. Search out pictures or visit stately homes for inspiration. You may also be able to visit one of the many restoration projects taking place in city parks in the UK, which are bringing these magnificent structures back to life. If you have the space, a mini greenhouse with a wooden frame can be painted in the same colour as your walls and sets the scene on a tiny scale. If space is even tighter, try sets of domed glass cloches and bell jars, which will not only protect young plants but immediately conjure up images of a Victorian walled kitchen garden. Terrariums also have a classic look. Fill one with moss, small pebbles and miniature plants to evoke the traditional gardening style first pioneered by 19th century plant-hunters, such as botanist James Ward. He invented the Wardian Case for transporting his valuable horticultural treasures on the long voyages back from his expeditions. Use glass containers, jars and vases to customise and create your own Wardian Cases or terrariums, or purchase DIY kits from online companies, who will supply everything you need.

Planting for a classical style

To achieve a classic look in beds and borders, grow climbing roses and sweet peas up metal obelisks and install tiered plant stands to display your flowers at different levels on a terrace or patio. A butler's tray is perfect for the tiniest of spaces and can be used to display a few plants potted up individually, or use the tray itself as a shallow planter for alpines and succulents.

Complete the theme by painting exterior walls and furniture in traditional muted shades. A combination of cast iron or painted metal furniture, and oak trestle tables and benches also help to set the scene. Dress them up with cushions and table linen in faded chintzy fabrics and add a candelabra and glass bowls of cut flowers to create a classic romantic design.

RIGHT **The White Garden at Sissinghurst Castle** in Kent in England, designed by Vita Sackville-West in the 1950s, is the epitome of elegant classic style, a look that still looks fresh today.

RIGHT **Copy the original plant hunters** and create terrariums in large glass jars to create a set of mini gardens that work inside and out. Ensure you take off the lids or keep them ajar to allow air to enter and escape.

BELOW **A traditional teak bench** in the decorative style of Sir Edwin Lutyens is a permanent investment and will last for years if the wood is correctly cared for.

CONTEMPORARY STYLE

Selecting the props and plants for a modern, of-the-moment outdoor space is quite easy. Stay abreast of current trends, and look at what the big brands in fashion and interiors are doing. Also check out the work of young garden designers at the major annual flower shows.

The gardening style gurus and horticultural taste-makers often follow trends in fashion and interior design, and you can keep your finger on the pulse by doing likewise. Look at the fashion colour of the year as a guide for your garden design if you want to stay on trend.

In contrast to the world of fast, throw-away fashion, however, gardening injects a sense of permanence. It is expensive and impractical to change heavy containers and outdoor furniture every year, but easy to ring the changes with smaller accessories. If you know you are moving on and are only looking for temporary fixes, then a selection of brightly coloured pots, woven plastic baskets and shopping bags will offer an inexpensive yet effective way of injecting modernity into your planting schemes.

Looking sharp

Contemporary style is about clean lines, minimal clutter and the use of asymmetrical geometry. A design laid out on an angle of 45 degrees, for example, can be enough to change the dynamic of a small area. Modern styles are often pared back to the barest bones, and as much attention is given to the hard landscaping as to the plants. Smooth, hewn stone, transparent reinforced

glass panelling and horizontal fencing with no obvious gaps or joins all create a seamless look, which can also give the impression of a space looking bigger than it really is.

To achieve a contemporary style, pay attention to the detail. It is important to use high-end, top quality materials throughout. Choose those that do not age too quickly and ensure the execution of any hard landscaping is perfect – any cracks or blisters in joints between paving stones will stand out like a sore thumb.

Pots and containers in materials similar to the hard landscaping add to the effect, with spots of colour introduced through furniture, soft furnishings and accessories. Plastic or melamine

ABOVE: **Geometric shapes** and modern materials are the key to designing a garden in a contemporary style. OPPOSITE PAGE CLOCKWISE FROM TOP LEFT **Concrete planters** work well against austere exposed brickwork in this modern space. **Corten steel** is a favourite material of many modern garden designers, chosen for its handsome looks and durability. **This roof terrace** at the back of a townhouse has a minimalist 21st century design. **Clean lines,** pale stone paving and metal garden furniture are enhanced by the restrained plant palette of mostly greens in this elegant garden.

furniture comes in a vast array of colours and styles, and it is durable, easy to maintain and light to carry up stairs to balconies and roof terraces. Bold, bright prints on cushion and table linen fabric, and hammered-metal accessories, including tin pots, which can be found in just about every shade, also allow you to mix and match primary colours to achieve an up-to-the-minute, contemporary look.

Industrial aesthetics

If using too much colour feels overwhelming, stick to zinc or corten steel. These materials work particularly well in converted industrial spaces. Former warehouses and factories that have been transformed into new homes lend

themselves to a particular aesthetic. Salvaged office furniture will not feel out of place here. Try using metal file boxes and small cabinets on wheels as containers; they can be planted up directly or pot up your flowers in plastic containers that can be dropped into them.

Wire-mesh shelving and wall racks can provide homes for faux-concrete pots, making the most of vertical spaces; ladders do the same job. Outdoor mirrors will help to make a tiny balcony appear larger, and they can be softened with clear fairy lights strung up on invisible wires that reflect in the glass. Also hang LED lanterns from hooks in your flowerbeds to show off the plants at night. Use battery-operated lights if you have no outdoor power supply.

OPPOSITE, LEFT **A sculptural water feature** is surrounded by verdant planting which prevents it from looking too stark.

OPPOSITE, RIGHT **Tightly clipped topiary**, such as these box balls, and spotlessly clean paving is key to pulling off a contemporary style successfully.

ABOVE **Planted with a mix** of evergreens, this street-facing balcony provides year-round interest for both the inhabitants of the apartment and passers-by.

LEFT **Bold pops of primary colours** can be injected into a design through the use of accessories, seating and other furnishings.

Modern planting styles

Architectural plants with a defined shape and form come into their own in a contemporary space. Cloud-pruned topiary makes a modern statement and you can clip almost any small-leaved evergreen shrub or tree into a desirable

ABOVE, LEFT **Red hot pokers** (*Kniphofia*) make an eye-catching addition to a contemporary scheme.
ABOVE, RIGHT **This rectangular timber** planter is enhanced by the uniform planting around the edges.
OPPOSITE, CLOCKWISE FROM TOP LEFT **Silver-leaved *Nepeta*** and *Artemisia* are offset by the scalloped foliage of *Alchemilla mollis*. **Layers of planting** in this modern scheme highlight contrasts in the various plants' form, colour and texture. ***Agapanthus*** and ***Euphorbia*** provide leaf structure and texture in a small modern space.

shape. Also try the large leaves and tall flower spikes of bears' breeches (*Acanthus mollis*), which will add drama to a border or deep planter, as will many grasses. Leafy hostas and ferns are perfect for modern containers in shady spaces, their foliage helping to soften the pots' edges.

If you choose to add colour, try red hot pokers (*Kniphofia*), available in orange and yellow, and the funnel-shaped scarlet flowers of *Crocosmia* 'Lucifer', which look stunning in oversized planters. For smaller containers, annual zinnias and cosmos come in bright zingy colours, and they are easy to grow from seed. For year-round contemporary planting, succulents are ideal for table-top planters or in vertical schemes, where they will require little maintenance or watering.

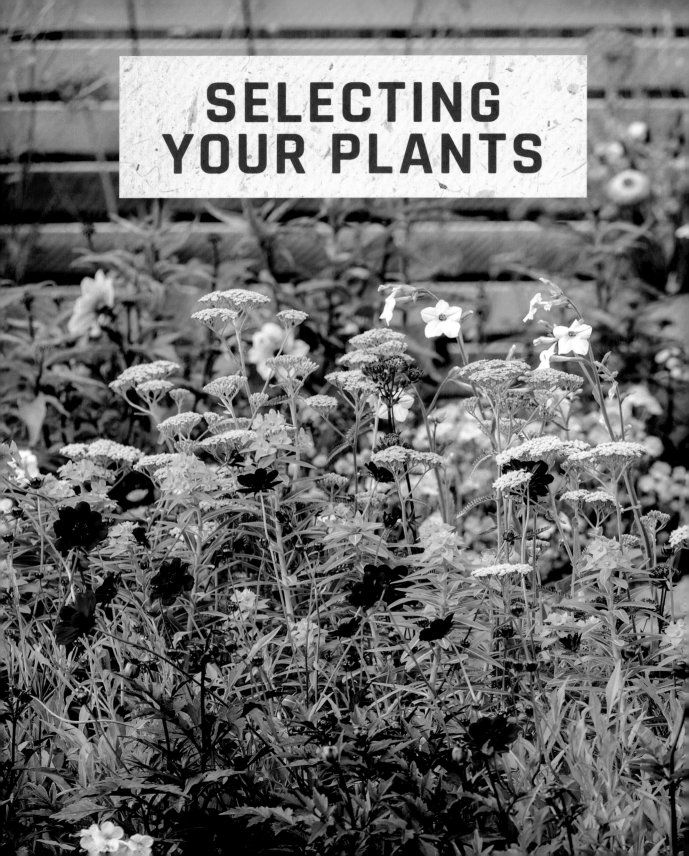

SELECTING
YOUR PLANTS

PLANNING BEFORE PLANTING

Before you spend any money on plants, my advice is to give yourself some time to plan where and what you would like to grow. Checking that a plant will suit its chosen site and soil, as well as its function within your design scheme, is essential.

When putting together a planting scheme, first do some research and draw up a wish list. On a warm spring day when you want to be working outside, it can be very tempting to start a project by rushing off to the nearest garden centre and buying an array of mature flowering plants already in full flush. Although this will give you some instant gratification and temporary pleasure, it is the most expensive and least satisfying way to garden, and is likely to lead to disappointment if the plants are already nearing or just past their best. I have had my head turned many a time by a bright seasonal display and, while I am still a sucker for the occasional spontaneous purchase, I have learnt that a little patience and forethought goes a long way and saves money in the long run.

The early summer and midsummer projects for this book were planned three to six months ahead of time. I had a pretty clear idea of what I wanted to grow and which containers I would

be using and I grew as much as possible from seed. The difference in price between a packet of seeds, from which you can grow many individual plants, and those that are fully grown is enormous. You can either pay a nursery or garden centre to do the work for you, or do it yourself – I personally find growing plants myself much more satisfying.

Sowing success

I used to think that raising flowers from seed would be too fiddly and time-consuming, but the more I do it, the more I realise that it is actually very straightforward. You will need to set aside some time, but it is really easy and offers you the chance to grow a wider range of plants and flowers and to inject your own personality into your planting schemes.

Many of the cottage-garden, old-fashioned blooms that I love to grow for my floristry work are not easily available at the garden centre, but their seeds can be purchased from independent specialist suppliers. Once you have grown them the first year, you can then collect the seeds from the flowers to resow the following year and make your plants really earn their keep (*see pp.84-85 for advice on how to sow seeds*).

ABOVE **Growing your own** plants from seed requires patience but it is the most rewarding way to garden. LEFT **Visiting flower markets** gives you ideas of what to grow yourself in a small cutting patch.

THE VALUE OF TREES

If you are lucky enough to have the space, I would urge you to plant a small tree or two. The more trees we plant collectively in our urban gardens, the more we will be contributing to the long-term health of our planet and the kinder we are being to ourselves and each other.

Trees provide elegant structural features in small urban gardens, and while we may include them for their beauty, they also fulfil a range of important ecological functions. Trees are vital to the environment. In built-up areas they significantly improve the air quality by absorbing pollution. They capture carbon and tap the soil for nutrients that are then recycled back into the earth as fallen leaves. They help to moderate climatic changes too, and just one tree can provide local flood protection. In hot weather trees function as natural air conditioners and keep our towns and cities cooler, while in winter, they act as insulators, protecting buildings and people from extremes in temperature.

Although you may think planting one tree will not make much of a contribution, if you multiply the number of single trees that could be grown in every small front or back garden, they soon add up and will make a huge difference.

Not only will a tree provide shade, privacy, shelter and a sense of security, but when used as part of a wider planting scheme, it also acts as a feature point or full stop. A tree encourages us to look up and beyond our immediate surroundings – something we often neglect to do. And when we lift our eyes to the sky, our personal awareness of our place in the world is heightened; a tree can literally be quite grounding. Select a variety that has year-round appeal, offering blossoms in spring, coloured foliage and fruit in autumn, and a striking outline in winter.

Decorative trees

When selecting a tree for your garden, do your homework and ensure you choose the right tree for the right place – it will save you making an expensive mistake. A tree costs a lot more than a packet of seeds so choose carefully. Look at small trees growing in your neighbourhood – any planted tree pits will also show what will thrive beneath them – and familiarise yourself with the names of a few favourites.

If I had to choose just one tree for a small city garden it would be the all-performing *Amelanchier lamarckii*, with its white starry flowers followed by summer fruits, and gorgeous bronze-tinged new foliage that turns a deeper red colour in the autumn. I also love the bright white-stemmed Himalayan birch (*Betula utilis* var. *jacquemontii*). Others worth considering are crab apples (*Malus*), rowans (*Sorbus*) and hawthorns (*Crataegus*), which all produce bee-friendly blossom in spring and autumn fruits to feed the birds.

OPPOSITE **Trees are vital** to the health of our planet and our personal well-being.
RIGHT **A mature urban** garden with several small trees creates a beautiful green sanctuary in the city.
BELOW RIGHT **Espaliered trees** trained along wires fixed to walls and fences make leafy backdrops.
BELOW LEFT **A Himalayan birch tree** is a living artwork with its exquisite papery gleaming white bark.

SHRUBS FOR SMALL SPACES

Annual and perennial flowers may be the stars of the show, but shrubs will provide structure, form and colour when other plants have faded. Look for shrubs that perform in each season, and offer handsome foliage, colourful stems, or pretty flowers that sustain year-round interest.

If you have a group of pots, it is a good idea to devote one to a shrub that has a permanent presence and can provide a backdrop to the other seasonal flowers as they come and go, offering interest when little else is in bloom.

You can clip and shape slow-growing evergreens yourself or splash out on some pre-trained topiary that will give your space instant definition. Many garden designers opt for evergreen box balls and cubes (*Buxus sempervirens*) because they are so well-behaved and easy to maintain. Box needs a yearly hair-cut but otherwise makes few demands; just keep an eye out for the fungal disease box blight, which causes the leaves to yellow and die. Boxed-leaved holly (*Ilex crenata*) is a good alternative if blight strikes. Its small glossy green leaves are equally good for clipping and it retains its shape for a long period. Both provide a green foil in a mixed planting scheme or a strong visual focus.

Flowering shrubs for small spaces include *Hydrangea macrophylla*, which has year-round appeal – its dried flower heads remain on the plant in winter and also make beautiful indoor displays. Mexican orange blossom (*Choisya ternata*) is another good choice for a container – I use both the flowers and foliage in my arrangements.

TOP **Shrubs with colourful** spring flowers in containers bring spots of seasonal colour to small spaces.
ABOVE **The lime green bracts** of a *Euphorbia* in spring are a head-turner in a municipal planting scheme.
OPPOSITE, CLOCKWISE FROM TOP LEFT **A dwarf lilac tree** offers delicious scent in early summer. **Hydrangea macrophylla** summer blooms add drama. **Honey spurge** (*Euphorbia mellifera*) has scented flowers as well as finger-like foliage. **Mexican orange blossom** (*Choisya ternata*) makes the perfect filler for a mixed bouquet. **Rock roses** (*Cistus*) produce papery flowers all summer. **Clipped box balls** offer evergreen structure and form.

CHOOSING CLIMBERS

In a small, enclosed space, climbing plants are some of your best allies; I would much prefer to see a wall or fence covered in glossy green ivy leaves than left bare and soulless. Create a verdant backdrop by clothing courtyard, patio or garden boundaries with beautiful climbers.

Evergreen climbers, such as ivy, are a good choice for small spaces, as they offer year-round colour and the perfect habitat for birds and other wildlife. Ivy also attaches itself to its host surface with tiny rootlets and requires no help from you to climb. Climbing hydrangeas (*Hydrangea anomala* subsp. *petiolaris*) do this too, and although they are deciduous and much slower growing, they provide an elegant background when fanned out against walls, and do not cause any damage to mortar. Perfect for growing where little else will thrive, they bear heads of lacy white flowers in summer and will cover a dark wall with beautiful heart-shaped bright green foliage for six months of the year.

Support systems
Most other climbing plants need an artificial support to help them climb. You can install trellis or horizontal panelled fencing on your boundary and plant climbers about 25–30cm (10–12in) from it to create a green wall. If installing trellis is not feasible, fix evenly-spaced horizontal wires to walls and fences or buy individual plant supports to use over or behind large containers.

You may have to tie the stems of climbing plants on to their supports at first, but in the majority of cases, they will soon start climbing on their own, their twining stems twisting and coiling around anything they touch. Roses are an exception, and even mature stems will need to be tied on to a support, unless they are weaving through a shrub or tree, where their thorns will hook onto the branches to help them climb.

On balconies and terraces plant a selection of flowering climbers, such as clematis, passion flowers and honeysuckle. In a larger space, try growing them through a tree or tall shrub; I like to thread clematis through rose bushes too. You can create a co-ordinated look by painting trellis, fencing and other outdoor woodwork in the same colour; paints and stains will also prevent these features from rotting if applied every year or two.

ABOVE **Ivy creates a verdant** backdrop, attaching itself to any surface; cut it back annually to keep it in check. OPPOSITE, CLOCKWISE FROM TOP LEFT **Climbing roses** entwined with clematis is a classic combination. **Rosa 'Blush Rambler'** is perfect for a tiny space, with flowers reminiscent of wild roses found in hedgerows. **Climbing hydrangeas** will grow rampantly to clothe the walls of a house or shed with their large white blooms. **Chinese wisteria** (*Wisteria sinensis*) puts on an annual spectacle of pendent sweetly perfumed purple or white blooms.

GRASSY EFFECTS

Grasses are the stalwarts of the urban garden. Evergreens offer year-round colour, while the leaves, flowers and seedheads of deciduous types provide late summer and autumn interest. Their rustling stems help camouflage background city noise, too, and the effect is wonderfully calming.

Grasses offer the urban gardener many benefits. As well as providing colour and texture, they are incredibly tactile and it's hard to resist reaching out to stroke their feathery plumes, which helps to soothe my frayed nerves after a stressful day.

Grasses may be the comfort blanket of the plant world, but they are also blessed with striking good looks and work hard to earn their place in a small space. Some, such as the stunning *Anemanthele lessoniana,* are evergreen; its tall arching clumps of foliage actually turn from green to a beautiful coppery palette of oranges, yellows and reds in the autumn and winter. Many others, including *Miscanthus* and some *Pennisetum,* are deciduous. If you have room, plant a selection. Try the compact *Miscanthus sinensis* 'Starlight', which bears pebble-hued fluffy tufts in autumn on hip-height mounds of thin silvery leaves, or opt for

Pennisetum alopecuroides 'Cassian's Choice', which replicates the sound of running water when its leaves rustle and sway. The dried stems and seedheads of deciduous grasses overwinter too.

Pots of plumes

Since all grasses have shallow root systems, they do well in pots and containers. You need to check their heights, however, as some can grow up to two metres (7ft) tall – ideal for screening but they would look out of place in a window box. If space is tight, then mix a packet of *Briza media* seed with some annual flowers. This gorgeous little plant, known as quaking grass, is a semi-evergreen with tiny teardrop flowers that bob in the breeze above a clump of green foliage. A favourite among flower-arrangers, it dries well and self-seeds profusely – I now have it growing all around my garden from one initial planting.

Another bonus is that grasses require little maintenance. In spring, simply comb through evergreens with your fingers or a kitchen fork to remove any dead stems, and cut down deciduous species to the ground – they will soon shoot up again to fill the gap. Grasses can become addictive and I recommend buying them from specialist growers, who offer the widest choice.

ABOVE **Quaking grass** (*Briza media*) is incredibly easy to grow from seed. Its tear-shaped flower heads look like little water droplets when they catch the light.
OPPOSITE **The tall plumes** of the Korean feather reed grass (*Calamagrostis brachytricha*) make you want to reach out and stroke them. Their gentle rustling in the breeze helps to soften the background noise of the city.

IDENTIFYING ANNUALS, BIENNIALS & PERENNIALS

Once you start growing your own flowers you will soon learn how they fall into different groups. There are three main categories, which reflect a plant's particular habit and lifespan, and knowing what's what will help you to choose those that best suit your space and chosen design.

Annuals

Many of the flowers that I grow from seed are known as "annuals". Sweet peas are a good example. These plants complete their whole life cycle within one year, germinating and putting on enough growth to flower profusely and set seed again within 12 months or less. One of the best reasons for growing annuals in small spaces, particularly in pots, is because they put all their energy into forming flowers rather than developing deep roots and therefore require shallow planting. Pot-grown plants also tend to flower more quickly as the compost warms up faster than the soil. Annual container planting keeps things exciting too – when a display is past its prime you can remove or hide it and bring something else to the fore to shake things up.

Annuals are split into two types: hardy and half-hardy. Hardy annuals survive temperatures below freezing and can be sown in autumn or spring. If it is very cold, a hardy annual planted in the autumn will become dormant in winter and only start growing again when it warms up. Half-hardy plants need to be protected from cold weather and die when temperatures hit freezing. Either sow their seeds when all risk of frost has passed, or start them off indoors on a windowsill.

Biennials

These plants form roots and foliage in the first year after germinating, and then flower and set seed the following year. Good examples of biennials are wallflowers and foxgloves. Seed packets will indicate whether plants are annual or biennial and offer guidance on sowing them. I grow both, but if you are only creating a temporary garden, then stick to annuals and you will reap the rewards more quickly.

Perennials

Flowering plants that live for more than two years are known as "perennials". They can be divided into two groups: "short-lived", which survive for about three or four years, and "long-lived", which generally live for at least five years. Perennials can also be tender or hardy. A tender perennial will not survive temperatures below freezing. The top growth of most hardy types dies back in the winter while the roots survive underground. Many perennials spread over time, so you need to check these details on the plant labels if you are planning to use them in pots or tiny spaces. You can also dig up clumps and split perennials in autumn or spring to make more plants. If you wish to create a temporary

container display, treat your perennials as annuals, removing them after they have set seed and transplanting them elsewhere.

Perennial plants with a tendency to self-seed are true-gift-givers. Even if you haven't time to collect and resow seed yourself, there are a huge number of plants that will save you the bother. Aquilegias and *Verbena bonariensis* will self-seed in every nook and cranny available – to the point where you are editing them out and donating them to your friends and neighbours. If you allow nature to give a helping hand you will end up with a space that looks completely naturalistic, even in the middle of a city.

Interlocking swathes of perennials, known as prairie planting, has become hugely fashionable over the last few years. Look at schemes by Piet

OPPOSITE **Annuals grown from seed**, such as scabious, will spread around if the seed heads are left to mature.
ABOVE LEFT **Foxgloves are biennial** plants but they self-seed to provide flowers year after year.
ABOVE RIGHT **A mixed scheme** of astrantias shows several different-coloured varieties of this perennial.

Oudolf, such as the High Line in New York, or Sarah Price's planting at the Olympic Park in London, for ideas on how these perennial designs work. The trick is to choose a small number of different species that suit your site and soil, then set them out in groups of the same type, and repeat these throughout the garden. The result looks very naturalistic, and can be a sustainable way of gardening in a small urban space.

SOWING FROM SEED

The easiest way to grow hardy plants from seed is to sow where you want them to grow, but raising them in pots indoors can increase your success rate.

Direct sowing

If you sow hardy annuals, such as *Ammi majus*, larkspur, scabious, cornflowers (above) and love-in-a-mist, in autumn they will be in flower by early summer the following year. When sowing in spring, wait until the soil surface is warm to the touch. In either case, make shallow drills with a cane and sprinkle seeds thinly directly onto the soil. Then cover them with a little more soil (check seed packs for recommended planting depths). This method allows you to clearly see the difference between your flowers when they emerge and weed seedlings.

When sowing half-hardy annuals and perennials directly outside, wait until there are no frosts. This applies to cosmos, tobacco plants, China asters, and didiscus.

Sowing in pots indoors

To steal a march on germination times you can start both hardy and half-hardy annuals on a windowsill indoors, alongside perennials such as astrantias, penstemons and dianthus (*see right*). Keep them under cover until any chance of frost has passed and transfer them outdoors for a few hours each day until the weather is warm enough to also leave them out at night.

STEP-BY-STEP

How to plant from seed

If you are sowing indoors you can buy seed trays and mini troughs, or recycle plastic fruit punnets, egg boxes or even ice-cube trays. Also try yoghurt pots and takeaway coffee cups for individual seeds, and in all cases use good quality seed compost. For convenience, and because I like its bright colour, I am using a plastic trough with a built-in water reservoir for these German pinks (*Dianthus carthusianorum*) and I have also transplanted some seedlings into small pots. Wild flowers in their native habitat in Europe, these pinks also suit containers in an urban space. They are members of the carnation family but with smaller, compact flower heads that are deliciously scented, as well as being edible. Sow these hardy perennials under cover between late autumn and late winter or early spring for a lovely show of blooms in the summer.

1.

- Fill the trough almost up to the rim with seed compost.
- Press down the compost gently to form a level surface. Using a pencil, or your finger, trace along the centre to create a depression roughly 1cm (⅓in) deep. Sprinkle seed thinly into the depression.

2.

- Smooth the compost over the seeds and then cover with a layer of vermiculite to help keep them moist. Label with the plant name.
- Place the seed trough in a light, warm area indoors, such as a windowsill, but keep your seedlings out of direct sunlight.

3.

- Water gently and regularly but do not flood. On this tiny planting scale, I find it easier to use a misting bottle or spray, rather than a watering can or jug, in order to control the water distribution and to avoid dislodging the seeds.

4.

- Germination will usually take place to great excitement within ten days to two weeks.
- When the plants are about 5cm (2in) tall and have developed a few sets of leaves, thin them out by removing congested seedlings to create enough space for the remaining plants. Here I have left six evenly spaced seedlings in the trough, and transplanted the others to individual pots.

5.

- To transplant the excess seedlings, fill a few small pots with potting-on compost. Make a hole in the compost with your finger or a blunt pencil.
- Use a small spoon or a butter knife to remove the tiny roots without damaging them. Then, holding the seedling by its leaves, place it into the hole in the compost, firming around the roots gently. Moisten with a mister and label the pot.

6.

- I have used 6cm (2½in) peat-free fibre pots to transplant my dianthus. These can eventually be planted in their entirety directly into the ground or into a much larger pot.
- Keep your seedlings undercover until the frosts have passed, and transfer them outdoors for a few hours each day until the weather is warm enough to leave them out day and night.

BUYING SEEDLINGS & BEDDING PLANTS

Although I try to grow as much as possible from seed, limited time and space inevitably means I am unable to cultivate everything myself. My next option is to buy seedlings or young plants, known as plugs, which I grow on, or bedding that offers instant gratification.

Seeking out seedlings

There are many specialist growers and nurseries that supply mail-order seedlings, and it is more economical to buy a box of baby plants and nurture them yourself than to purchase them fully grown. Seek out online companies or visit those open to the public; some are open for a few days each year to showcase new varieties. For inspiration, you can also visit open gardens, such as The Beth Chatto Garden and Great Dixter, which have nurseries attached to them.

Other sources of seedlings are local plant fairs or gardening neighbours who may have some surplus. If you are in London, Columbia Road Flower Market is well worth a visit, but most street and farmers markets offer a good selection and provide an opportunity to chat to the growers who can offer you advice.

Filling gaps with bedding

There is a certain amount of snobbery in the horticultural world attached to so-called bedding plants. They are really a mix of annuals and short-lived, often tender, perennials bred especially for their colourful displays, and they are ideal for pots, containers, hanging baskets and gaps in flowerbeds. They include begonias, petunias and busy lizzies, which you will recognise as the decorative summer plants seen in city parks and town centres, where they are generally planted together in a froth of vibrant multi-coloured mixtures.

For the purposes of creating harmonious, elegant designs, it is tempting to dismiss bedding, but these plants can be worth their weight in gold if you use them sparingly as fillers in pots, or pick out a carefully edited selection of trailing varieties to create your own beautifully styled hanging garden (*see project on pp.144-145*). The benefit of bedding is its long flowering period, offering displays that continue up to the first frosts in autumn. You will find a good selection for sale at your local garden centre, DIY store, or supermarket, which will be ready for planting outside in early summer. If you can resist them when they first appear, you can often pick them up for much lower prices later in the season.

ABOVE **Pots of seasonal bedding** plants offer the opportunity to create an instant garden.
RIGHT **Flower markets,** such as this famous one at Columbia Road in East London, allow you to buy plants directly from growers, and offer a more cost-effective way of purchasing lots of plants for a new garden.

GROWING BULBS, CORMS, RHIZOMES & TUBERS

Harbingers of spring, bulbs bring colour to the garden when little else is in bloom. Some bulbs flower in late summer and autumn, helping to fill gaps that appear at this time of year, while a hardy few show their faces in the depths of winter, shrugging off the snow and ice.

Starting with snowdrops in late winter and following through with a succession of daffodils, grape hyacinths (*Muscari*), bluebells and tulips – these familiar flowers of the spring garden herald the new start of the gardening year and its boundless possibilities.

What is a bulb?

A bulb is essentially an energy storage unit, made up of fleshy, fibrous material with a growing point at its centre. Think of an onion cut in half lengthways and you will get the picture. If you leave an onion for long enough in the vegetable rack it will start to grow thin green leaves of its own accord, and this is what a bulb does underground. If you plant an onion once it has sprouted, it will indeed form a flowering stem, just like its beautiful cousins, the pompom-flowered ornamental alliums.

Corms, rhizomes and tubers, while different in appearance and structure to a bulb – a rhizome, for example, is a swollen underground stem – are all food stores and perform in a similar way to produce their flowers and leaves.

Bulbs come in a variety of shapes and sizes and, generally speaking, the larger the bulb the bigger the flower head, so if space is at a premium, take this into consideration. But limited room does not mean it is impossible to grow bulbs; it is more a question of how many and what you grow them in. Left to their own devices, many bulbs want to "naturalise", which means they will multiply and spread themselves around. A profusion of flowering bulbs looks fantastic in a wide, open space or a woodland glade – there is nothing more stunning in early spring than a carpet of crocuses pushing their little heads through the soil. In a small area, however, the answer is to grow them in pots, which you can swap around as one type fades and another comes into bloom. Or plant a single large pot as a 'bulb lasagna' made up of different layers, where one species will flower directly after another to provide a continuous display.

Planting times

Just as you need to think a few months ahead when planting seeds, you must plan in advance for bulbs. Spring- and early summer-flowering bulbs should be planted from autumn to early winter, and plant those that bloom in midsummer and autumn in spring. You will see sacks or bags of spring bulbs in supermarkets and garden centres from late summer onwards,

and this is the time to start planning. Scented hyacinths forced indoors for early flowering are very easy to grow (*see project on pp.160-161*) and you can do the same thing with grape hyacinths (*Muscari*), which look lovely potted individually in a row. Deep bowls of paperwhites and other miniature daffodils, followed by snake's head fritillaries, will take you through to late spring. Follow these with a pot of perfumed lily-of-the-valley. Given as a traditional gift to celebrate May Day in Europe, if you leave it on the doorstep or in a stairwell the blooms will fill you with pleasure as you come and go. For a larger display, pack a punch with tulips planted in a big zinc container or wooden planter. Mix two or three varieties in harmonious colourways – 'Black Parrot', 'Queen of Night' and 'Burgundy' produce an intoxicating wine-coloured combination.

Late-season blooms

Bulbs in summer and autumn have more competition from other blooms, although dahlias do their best to stand out from the crowd and provide a great show of exotic-looking flowers. Alliums, especially the smaller-headed *Allium sphaerocephalon* or drumstick variety, are good for small spaces as they are tall and slender.

OPPOSITE **A drift of bulbs**, including dwarf narcissi and crocuses, welcomes in the spring.
ABOVE LEFT **Mini pots** of grape hyacinths (*Muscari*) suit a tiny garden space.
ABOVE **Purple pompoms** of alliums make great cut fresh or dried flowers.
LEFT *Tulipa* **'Queen of Night'** is perfect for a moody, sultry effect.

Agapanthus remind me of seaside resorts, but they work equally well in an urban environment, particularly in containers, as they like nothing better than being wedged tightly against each other. *Crocosmia,* with their burnt orange or red hues, bridge the gap between summer and autumn. They grow like a weed in my garden so need to be watched, but one or two corms will quickly form a clump and provide a dazzling colour combination when grown among dahlias in similar tones, such as 'Jescot Julie' and 'New Baby'. Although autumn tends to make me feel wistful, I am convinced that a bright show of colour at the end of the growing season is nature's way of keeping our spirits high.

ADDING SCENT TO YOUR SCHEME

For me, flowers and scent go hand in hand and I always include perfumed plants in my schemes. Sadly, the cut flower and horticultural industries seem to have made fragrance a bit of an afterthought, but there are still many gorgeous flowers that you can grow to fill your garden with scent.

I find it bewildering that scent is not one of the qualities plant breeders focus on when creating new plant ranges. Disease-resistance and bright colours seem to have become the holy grail for commercial growers, and many flower varieties produced for the mass market have lost their true scent through genetic manipulation.

Timeless perfumes

Historically, flowering plants brought us the first bottled perfumes and the use of plants in toiletries and cosmetics is age-old. They provided the scented oils and waters that were used as part of the ritual of adornment; the first lifestyle accounts on papyrus scrolls detail the harnessing of natural fragrances to cleanse the body and anoint the spirit.

From every culture since the Ancient Egyptians, plants and herbs have been used for their hygienic, medicinal and psychological benefits. Archaeological finds have unearthed ornate amphora or oil jars still impregnated with the original scent, which show how perfume was revered as a precious commodity. A gift from and to the gods, it was used to embalm bodies to ensure a peaceful afterlife. Incense, the natural resin from the *Boswellia* or frankincense tree,

was harvested in its pure form, while the earliest manufactured perfumes were derived from the crushed and blended leaves and petals of scented flowers, before the first distillation processes were introduced in the 11th century.

The use of perfume for personal, religious and cultural purposes has always been with us and our powerful response to scent is wired into our brains. Our noses are incredibly sensitive and our sense of smell is many times more developed than our sense of taste. Linked directly to the limbic lobe of the brain where we also register emotions and memory, scents often evoke past events or places. Vivid recollections are reawakened by a smell already in our memory bank, based on childhood associations with the natural world. Equally, some perfumes just make us feel happy or at peace.

Given that it is no longer a requisite for daily survival, we are perhaps in danger of losing our full capacity to smell and there is a growing disconnect between flowers, their perfume and our ability to recognise them. Today's cheap synthetic fragrances are largely bland and less a gift from the gods or Mother Nature and more a marketing dream. Growing your own flowers, however, goes some way to reversing this trend.

Fill your space with perfume

The answer to solving the scent conundrum is to reconnect with perfume and choose to grow plants for their fragrance as well as their flowers. If you only have limited space, make sure that at least one flowering plant is a scented variety. Imagine you are creating your very own fragrance lab and track down those that give you a buzz when you smell them. Start by working out which synthetic scents appeal to you, such as lavender or rose, then familiarise yourself with their natural forms. Once you have identified those that bring you the most pleasure, you are on the road to becoming your own scent or aromatherapy practitioner.

Among the perfumed flowers I would choose for a small space, in no particular order, are scented-leaved pelargoniums, such as P. 'Attar of Roses' and P. 'Sweet Mimosa', tobacco plants (*Nicotiana*), pinks (*Dianthus*), violets (*Viola*), lily-of-the-valley (*Convallaria majalis*), wallflowers (*Erysimum*), irises (*Iris*) and stocks (*Matthiola*). To create a perfumed wall, try climbers, such as honeysuckle (*Lonicera*) and jasmine (*Jasminum officinale*). Finally, for winter perfume when we all need something particularly delicious to brighten our spirits, grow paper whites and hyacinths in pots (*see project on pp.160-161*).

OPPOSITE **White lilac** blooms inhaled up close will give you an instant high in spring.
TOP LEFT **Scented stocks** (*Matthiola longipetala*) help to fill a small space with heady early evening scent.
CENTRE LEFT **The fragrance** of the dainty lily-of-the-valley (*Convallaria majalis*) is a gift of the gods.
LEFT **The tiny petals** of sweet violets (*Viola odorata*) belie their intoxicating scent.

SELECTING FRAGRANT ROSES

Originally grown for their medicinal benefits, roses today are more commonly cultivated for their colourful flowers and intoxicating perfume. Some will bloom repeatedly throughout the summer and autumn, offering the urban gardener great value.

We only have to look at the original apothecary's rose (*Rosa gallica* var. *officinalis*) and its various uses for evidence that historically these plants were widely cultivated for medicinal purposes. Their fantastic looks were secondary in those days, but we now grow roses in our gardens primarily for their beauty and delicious scent. Look out for the *Rosa gallica* 'Versicolor' (above) – a magical, bi-coloured white and red striped rose that looks as if it is has been lifted from the pages of *Alice in Wonderland*.

My obsession with rose scents began when I first started my floristry business. My intention was to offer bouquets of top quality, fresh roses, but I was disappointed to discover that most imported roses lose what little scent they may have after several weeks in cold storage. I began my quest to create a range of rose-scented products to accompany my bouquets, blending my own bath oils and candles in my kitchen. For a long while, the very fabric of the house seemed to be impregnated with the scent of roses, but it was only a couple of years ago that I took the plunge and started growing them in my garden.

Having always assumed that roses were fussy and difficult to grow and maintain, I have discovered the opposite is true, and I now realise that no flower garden, however tiny, is complete without at least one rose. More to the point, if you select a highly scented variety, one rose is all you need in an enclosed space.

I have selected some of my favourite scented roses on the opposite page. Others I would recommend include the white, repeat-flowering Susan Williams-Ellis, which has a traditional rose perfume; Summer Song, with its fruity floral-scented burnt orange flowers; and Sir Walter Scott – its blush-pink flowers and "old rose" perfume remind me of those my grandma grew.

GROWING ROSES

Roses enjoy a sunny site and fertile soil – dig well-rotted manure in before planting. Add mycorrhizal fungi to the planting hole to help the roots establish, and ensure the graft union (the bump at the base of the main stem) is at soil level and not buried. Prune roses annually in late winter or early spring to encourage them to bloom prolifically; check a reliable source, such as the Royal Horticultural Society's website (rhs.org.uk), for pruning advice, as each type of rose requires a different method.

Recommended scented roses

Here are some of the best scented roses for a small space. They will thrive in a large pot of John Innes No 3 compost or in a border, and the shrubs will grow to just over 1m (3ft) in height. All these roses flower prolifically and have the most delicious perfume.

Darcey Bussell
A deep dark red-flowered shrub rose with a sharp fruity scent that is not at all sweet or cloying – think apples and freshly mown grass.

Charlotte
The cupped-shaped blooms of this repeat-flowering shrub are a soft yellow and carry the oriental, musky fragrance of a classic tea rose.

Munstead Wood
Named after Gertrude Jekyll's own garden, the velvety crimson flowers invite you to bury your nose in them and enjoy their autumn fruit scent.

William and Catherine
The blooms of this shrub rose change over time from pale apricot to cream to white. Highly perfumed, the blooms have a fresh, herby, modern scent.

Félicité-Perpétue
This rambling rose produces an abundance of scented white pompon flowers, and the disease-resistant foliage is almost evergreen.

Ferdinand Pichard
A repeat-flowering rose with striking stripy petals, it is a direct descendant of the apothecary's rose, with an intense sweet fragrance.

Blush Noisette
Perfect for growing in pots, either as a small rambler up against a trellis or as a shrub rose. The small pale pink flowers have a strong spicy perfume.

Scent from Heaven
An award-winning rose that lives up to its name. The scent hints of summer fruits, and the apricot blooms turn a richer colour as they mature.

GROWING THERAPEUTIC FLOWERS

The power of plants to soothe the mind and body is well known, but experts are still not exactly sure why certain aromatic oils have a therapeutic effect. Nevertheless, it is a great idea to grow and use a few in your garden to enhance your sense of wellbeing.

The fragrances of certain plants have long been used as remedies to help us relax, calm our nerves, relieve tension and anxiety, aid sleep and, in some cases, alleviate depression. The centuries-old practice of aromatherapy involves inhaling these scents directly, bathing in their oils or massaging them into the skin. Therapeutic plants are also ingested in the form of a tea or tisane. Many are easy to grow in an urban garden, allowing you to take full advantage of their beneficial qualities.

Soothing lavender

To experiment with therapeutic plants in a small space I would suggest starting with a pot of lavender (*Lavendula*), a plant renowned for its aromatic qualities and as a powerful relaxant. It is extremely easy to grow in a container; its only requirement is plenty of sunshine. There are many varieties available and different types flower at different times throughout the summer and autumn, starting with the French lavenders early in the season and ending with those that fade with the first frosts. If the scent appeals to you, why not create a mini lavender garden with a colour scheme that ranges from pale lilac to deep purple? My favourite variety and one

of the best for impact in a small space is the English lavender, *Lavandula angustifolia* 'Hidcote'. Stunning as a single specimen, its deep violet, intensely perfumed flower spikes appear above a neat mound of silvery grey fragrant leaves, which scent the air and any clothing that brushes against them. I sometimes carry a stem of this in my pocket to bring out in moments of anxiety – sitting in a traffic jam nerves a-jangling, for example – and I often sleep with a couple of flower heads under my pillow case, so I can definitely vouch for this pretty plant.

CALMING LAVENDER SACHETS

Cut flowers after the blooms have faded, just above the green area of the stem. Ensure you do not cut into the brown woody part of the stem. Save the flowers heads and allow them to dry out in a vase with no water or put them in the airing cupboard to scent your linen. Use the dried flowers and leaves to fill muslin sachets and place these under your pillow or beneath a running bath tap.

△ **Chamomile (*Chamaemelum nobile*) is used** in aromatherapy for its calming properties. Grow its daisy-like flowers from young plants and dry them to make your own herbal tea, or sprinkle the contents of a tea bag over a seed tray filled with compost. Keep the tray watered in a warm place and seedlings will appear in a couple weeks. Both the flowers and foliage of chamomile have a fruity apple aroma, and plants can be used as part of a wildflower scheme or knitted together to form a carpet or "chamomile lawn". The plants flower all summer, providing blooms for tea and for picking and arranging. They self-seed profusely, too.

△ **Fennel (*Foeniculum vulgare*)** is another generous self-seeder that earns its keep with feathery scented foliage and seeds that offer many therapeutic benefits. Both the leaves and seeds, which appear after flowering, are edible and reputed to be good for the digestion. They also work well as a natural breath freshener. Fennel is tall plant, growing up to a metre (3ft) in height, but its clouds of wispy emerald leaves and bright yellow lacy umbels do not require much depth of soil, so it can be grown easily in a pot. The foliage has an aniseed scent and flavour, and the flowers smell like a bag of liquorice allsorts.

OPPOSITE **Heads of dried lavender** flowers keep their scent for months. RIGHT **Marigolds are easy to grow** from seed; their bright orange or yellow flower petals have myriad uses.

◁ **Pot marigold (*Calendula officinalis*)** has cheerful bright orange or yellow flowers but their scent is an acquired taste and you will either love it or hate it, so smell before buying. It's best know for its power to heal the skin and you can make your own cream by blending the petals with an emulsifier such as beeswax, together with glycerine and water. Simmer the mixture gently until it turns orange, and keep it in the fridge for treating burns, wounds and rashes. Very easy to grow in any soil and full sun, marigolds make a good cut flower. The petals are also edible and look fantastic in a green salad.

CHOOSING HERBS

There is some overlap between the plants used in aromatherapy remedies and those we define as herbs. Broadly speaking, herbs are plants whose leaves can be used in food, flavouring, medicine and perfume, and you can grow a wide variety in the tiniest of spaces.

Today, we associate herbs with their culinary rather than their medicinal uses, but in days gone by they were predominantly cultivated for their healing properties. Herb gardens were originally planted in the monasteries of medieval Europe where monks and nuns cared for the sick and established "officinae" or apothecaries, providing treatment to alleviate all manner of ailments. This eventually led to the opening of commercial pharmacies in cities where tisanes, tinctures and pastes were prepared and sold as cures. The Latin word *officinalis* following the genus name of a plant, such as sage, *Salvia officinalis*, denotes its original use as a medicine. It seems to me that it is no small coincidence that the plants with this nomenclature are also the mostly highly scented. Presumably it was their perfume that first drew healers to investigate their medicinal properties.

ABOVE **Creeping thyme** (*Thymus serpyllum*) has pretty pink flowers and aromatic foliage.
LEFT **A small raised bed** devoted to herbs is a must for any keen cook and will also provide year-round colour and fragrance.
RIGHT **Rosemary, mint and sage** are easy to grow in pots and all have therapeutic qualities.

CREATING A MINI APOTHECARY

The following herbs offer a pleasing combination of scents and flavours, which also work together as a well-considered purple-blue colour scheme. One plant of each variety in a shallow container or wall planter will provide you with enough choice for seasoning different types of food, preparing your own tisanes or blending perfumed bath salts and shower scrubs.

▽ **Rosemary (*Rosmarinus officinalis*)** bears small pin-like evergreen leaves and clusters of purple-blue flowers in late spring and early summer. One of the best-smelling herbs for an instant pick-me-up and natural cold remedy, plunge a sprig in boiling water to help clear the sinuses. It can also be used for flavouring many savoury dishes and is delicious in a palate-cleansing sorbet or ice cream. Grow rosemary in free-draining soil and a sunny site, and clip it after flowering to reinvigorate growth and keep the plant bushy. The clippings can be dried to make an aromatic potpourri. Thyme can be used for a similar effect. Its antiseptic qualities are good for soothing sore throats. Look for *Thymus* 'Silver Posie', a compact variety with tiny purple-pink flowers and silvery grey leaves. Crush the leaves between your fingers to release their scent.

ABOVE **Create a herb garden** in upcycled olive oil cans.
BELOW LEFT **Rosemary has astringent qualities** and can be used to alleviate colds. Recent research shows that it is also beneficial for memory retention.
BELOW RIGHT **Sage helps to boost concentration** and is now being used in trials to find a cure for dementia.

△ **Lemon Balm (*Melissa officinalis*)** is a widely available hardy perennial herb with a sharp lemony scent. Use the leaves in a tisane in times of stress to calm your nerves. Its nectar-rich flowers are a delicate pale purple and a favourite of bees, while its aromatic citronella fragrance is a useful natural mosquito deterrent. Lemon balm is very easy to grow in almost any soil and a sunny or part-shaded site, and it will spread and self-seed profusely. For an alternative herb with similar soothing properties, try lemon verbena (*Aloysia citrodora*), which also has citrus-scented leaves. Not as hardy as lemon balm, it may need winter protection in cold areas.

◁ **Sage (*Salvia officinalis*)** offers the perfect combination of year-round green-grey foliage and pretty blue-purple summer flowers, both of which are edible. This plant has a distinctive scent with an astringent quality – somehow you know it's going to do you good. Regarded as the king of herbs, it has a broad range of therapeutic properties. Sage tea, also known as the "thinkers' tea" - the clue is in its name – is thought to improve concentration and boost serotonin levels. Like rosemary, sage is a shrub and needs a free-draining soil and full sun to thrive. Cut it back after flowering to maintain a bushy shape.

△ **Mint (*Mentha* species)** There are a number of different varieties of mint, each with its own delightful qualities. Peppermint (*Mentha* x *piperita*), spearmint (*Mentha spicata*) and pineapple or apple mint (*Mentha suaveolens* 'Variegata') are all worth growing for their individual scents and flavours. As it tends to be a bit of a thug in all its forms, grow it separately in a container to prevent it taking over and swamping other plants. A dedicated mint wall planter of all three is a simple and inexpensive solution (*see herb project on pp.116-117*).

Of the three mints mentioned, peppermint has the strongest flavour and is ideal for making tea or cordial; spearmint is milder but delicious with vegetables or in salads; pineapple mint, not surprisingly, has a fruity mint taste that works well in desserts and fruit-flavoured drinks. In all cases, mint is known to aid digestion and promote peaceful sleep. Added to that, peppermint and spearmint plants produce pretty spikes of purple and pink flowers that attract bees. Pineapple mint boasts pale pink blooms and cream and green variegated foliage that contrasts well with the plain green varieties. All mints grow in any reasonable soil and sun or shade, and they will provide you with scent and taste while looking and doing you good too.

EXPERIMENTING WITH COLOUR

HARMONIOUS COLOURS

To save time and expensive mistakes, I recommend sticking to the basic precept of a fixed complementary colour scheme, using a set of shades that work together harmoniously. These are the hues that lie next to each other on the colour wheel opposite.

On the following pages, I show you how to create a collection of mini flower gardens using blooms in one or more colours that complement each other. For a small space, this is aesthetically pleasing and prevents it from becoming too busy. Another tip to create harmony is to repeat the same flower variety in shades of the same hue.

The queen of colour

I draw inspiration from the great gardener and designer Gertrude Jekyll when creating my colour schemes. Jekyll became famous during the late 19th and early 20th centuries for her beautiful planting style, which was based on a deep understanding of colour, acquired through her training and work as an artist. She outlines her theories on how to compose pictures with plants in her best-known book, *Colour Schemes for the Flower Garden*, first published in 1908 but still in print today by Frances Lincoln. The large gardens Jekyll designed offered the space to work with broad harmonious swathes of plants in subtle gradations of colour, creating borders of flower-filled perfection throughout the seasons. Her strength as an artist-gardener was to recognise the value of harmony while avoiding monotony – ideas we can use in our small city spaces today.

TOP **Gertrude Jekyll's ideas** for using flowers in brush strokes of colour can be adapted to suit small spaces. ABOVE **A colour scheme** in pink and burgundy is pleasing to the eye and restful, creating a calm scene. OPPOSITE **The colour wheel** made from freshly picked flowers and foliage demonstrates how colours that sit next to one another create harmonious combinations.

CHOOSING A COLOUR PALETTE

When putting together a palette of plants for your beds, borders and container displays, consider their colour, tonal variations, flower and leaf shapes and textures. Combine them in groups to create eye-catching contrasts, subtle blends and a balanced scheme.

Inspired by Gertrude Jekyll, I have put together a series of seasonal harmonious planting palettes, laid out like colour charts, to provide you with easy-to-use guides. Most city gardens are small and while many of us don't have the large borders of Jekyll's own garden at Munstead Wood in Surrey, where she put into practice her expansive planting palettes, we can distil and translate her ideas for 21st century urban spaces. If you only have a tiny planting area, or just a single container or window box, it is visually more pleasing to use shades within one colour range and restrict the number of plant varieties.

My take on her ideas is to colour-block on a miniaturised scale and the results are intended to represent a series of vignettes. Jekyll devised her gardens as "living pictures" and it is something along these lines that I am attempting to demonstrate. My suggestions show how to paint a picture using plants in containers, and they all are very easy to achieve, even if you are a first-time gardener. I have compiled a total of 14 different projects in five harmonious colourways, together with 14 complementary planting palettes that will introduce you to a host of other wonderful plant varieties, all of which are suitable for small spaces.

The power of colour

There is much anecdotal evidence to suggest that colour has an effect on our moods. For example, colours on the red-orange side of the spectrum are considered to be hot, with associations of excitement and vibrancy but with the possible undercurrent of anger and danger, which is why red is used as a warning signal. Blues and greens, by contrast, are thought to be calming colours that represent tranquility and serenity, but they can also convey a sense of melancholy.

When selecting a planting palette for your garden, you will probably know instinctively which colours appeal to you, but you can also be guided by those that reflect your choice of clothes or the interior décor of your home, which will provide a coordinated look inside and out.

ABOVE **The perennial wallflower** Erysimum 'Bowles's Mauve' is the backbone of the blue-mauve flower garden, as it is in flower almost all year round. OPPOSITE CLOCKWISE FROM TOP LEFT **Aquilegias,** Bulgarian honey garlic (Nectaroscordum siculum subsp. bulgaricum), cornflowers (Centaurea montana) and hardy geraniums make a lovely planting combination in late spring and early summer, with different forms, shapes and textures in shades that complement one another.

BURGUNDY & PINK

Contrast these pink and burgundy plants with moody blues and whites to welcome in summer with a profusion of pastel shades.

1 & 2 *Paeonia* (peony) is the family of plants that really catch the eye, with their big blowsy blooms. I love them all, but a favourite is *Paeonia lactiflora* **'Pure Delight'**, its frilly pale pink, double flowers remind me of a ballerina's tutu. Peonies' flowering season is quite short, so make the most of them by planting a second variety. For a more glamorous type, try *Paeonia lactiflora* **'Karl Rosenfield'** with its show-stopping deep magenta blooms. Grow them in sun and moist, free-draining soil. Heights & spreads: 90cm x 80cm (36in x 32in).

8

9

7

10

3 *Digitalis purpurea* (foxglove) is a UK native and each plant bears one or more flower spikes made up of many individual thimble-like blooms, with maroon freckles at their throats that look as if they have been painted on. These biennials add height and elegance to any planting scheme and are a huge attraction for bees. Grow them in shade and well-drained but moist soil. Height & spread: 1.2m x 60cm (4ft x 2ft).

4 *Centaurea cyanus* 'Black Boy' (cornflower) will help to tone down a largely pink colour scheme and prevent it from looking too sickly-sweet. For dark, near-black accents, this sun-loving annual does the job perfectly and it is easy to grow from seed in well-drained soil. Height & spread: 90cm x 15cm (3ft x 6in).

5 & 6 *Geranium* **Patricia** (cranesbill) is one of the many varieties of hardy geranium that fits into a pink summer scheme. 'Patricia' has brightly coloured blooms but if you are looking for a more muted hue, try *Geranium versicolor*, with its delicately striated petals. Both perennials grow well in sun or part shade and free-draining soil. Heights & spreads: 60cm (24in).

7 *Heuchera* **'Blackout'**, like most heucheras, is grown for its distinctive foliage. Its spreading mound of semi-evergreen dark leaves looks great in pots and the edges of well-drained beds in sun or part shade. The airy blooms are a bonus. Height & spread: 65cm x 50cm (26in x 20in).

8 & 9 *Papaver somniferum* **'Lauren's Grape'** and *Papaver orientale* **'Lauren's Lilac'** (poppy) fit beautifully into this palette and they are both stunning. Grow them from seed in poor, well-drained soil and sun, and they will then spread around. Also save the seedheads for use in dried arrangements. Height & spread: 50cm (30in).

10 *Allium sphaerocephalon* produces small oval flower heads on tall slim stems, and works well in a small space, towering over shorter plants. Although the flowers don't open until midsummer, they look fantastic while still in bud. Plant bulbs in autumn in well-drained soil and full sun. Height & spread: 90cm x 60cm (3ft x 2ft).

FLOWERING CRATES

If you have a low table, flat-bottomed chair or stool, dress it up with a vintage crate or shallow wooden box filled with a selection of dainty alpine plants and enjoy the intricate beauty of their blooms up close.

My old wooden table is the perfect height for displaying mounds of mossy saxifrages, allowing me to view these tiny plants in the detail they deserve. I am using a variety called *Saxifraga* 'Peter Pan', which produces claret-coloured buds that open to reveal tiny clusters of star-like flowers ranging from pale pink to dark burgundy. The natural habitat of this diminutive alpine – it reaches a height and spread of just 20-25cm (8-10in) – is a mountainside and it is often grown in the free-draining conditions of a rock garden or stone trough, but it is also perfect for this project. Unusually for an alpine, it tolerates some shade, and each plant will spread to form a lovely undulating evergreen carpet.

1. **Line your crate** or box with a sheet of thick plastic so that the edges overlap the top. This will prevent the compost falling through any gaps. Use scissors to make a few drainage holes in the plastic at regular intervals along the base.

2. **Fill with soil-based** potting compost, such as John Innes No 1, mixed with some horticultural grit. Spread it evenly so that it is level and reaches a couple of centimetres (1in) below the rim of the crate. Trim the plastic along the top of the crate.

3. **Remove the plants** from their plastic pots and lay them out on top of the compost so they are evenly spaced. I am using six here, but the number depends on the crate's size. Leave 10cm (4in) between each plant to allow space for growth.

4. **Loosen the roots** if they have become pot bound by gently teasing them out with your fingers. Then make a hole deep enough to accommodate. Insert the plant and firm in gently. Repeat with the remaining plants.

EXPERT TIP
Saxifrages like free-draining soil conditions, similar to their native mountainside habitat, so make sure your crates or containers have plenty of drainage.

5. **Dress the top** of the compost with pea shingle or stone chippings. These will help to keep the lower leaves of the plants dry and prevent them from rotting. Water the plants gently every other day, but take care not to overwater or flood them.

Early summer palette

RED & ORANGE

These hot, sizzling shades create a dramatic contrast with their green foliage and are guaranteed to brighten up any city space.

1 *Calendula officinalis* (pot marigold) is incredibly easy to grow in all soil types in full sun, either in beds or pots. It is a hardy annual but will self-seed and come back year after year. The orange flowers are great for cutting, and the petals are edible and good for scattering over salads. Height & spread: 60cm x 45cm (24in x 18in).

2 *Eschscholzia californica* 'Orange King' (California poppy) is one of the most rewarding annuals for a novice gardener, as it grows well in poor soils. In its native habitat you will see luminous swathes decorating the kerbsides. Sow the seeds in autumn and early spring in a sunny spot. Height & spread: 30cm x 10cm (12in x 4in).

3 *Thunbergia alata* (black-eyed Susan) has a distinctive black dot at the centre of its vibrant flower heads, which is how this sun-loving annual climber came by its common name. This twining, vine-like plant will scramble over a wigwam or plant support in a pot to produce a fantastic blaze of early summer colour with some height. Height & spread: 2.2m x 0.5m (8ft x 20in).

4 *Ranunculus asiaticus* **'Aviv Red'** (Persian buttercup) has frilly carmine flowers which bring a dazzling glow to the late spring garden. Grow it from corms planted the previous autumn in moist soil and full sun. Ranunculus also make fantastic cut flowers. Height & spread: 30cm x 15cm (12in x 6in).

5 *Alstroemeria* **'Flaming Star'** (Peruvian lily) has exotic origins but despite its tropical appearance it grows well in more northerly climes, althought it needs full sun to thrive. Most varieties will fit into this colour palette but 'Flaming Star' is one of the more flamboyant. Buy small plants in late spring for an instant show in early summer. Height & spread: 75cm x 45cm (30in x 18in).

6 *Berberis thunbergii* **'Lutin Rouge'** (barberry) is a pretty variety of this prickly, deciduous shrub. A compact plant with upright slender growth and fiery-coloured foliage, it is very easy to maintain. Plant it at the front of a sunny or lightly shaded border or in a large container. Height & spread: 45cm x 25cm (18in x 10in).

7 *Erysimum cheiri* **'Fire King'** is one of the earliest wallflowers to put on a show of brilliant colour and scent. Plant it with tulips for a knockout display. You can grow it from seed sown undercover in the autumn or pick up bare-rooted plants and plant these in free-draining soil and a sunny site in autumn for early summer blooms. Regular deadheading will prolong the flowering period. Strictly a biennial, replant it each year. Height & spread: 30cm (12in).

8 *Tulipa* **'Ballerina'** is one of my favourite tulips, not just because it happens to be scented. It is tall and elegant, with slim, lily-type flower heads and therefore doesn't tend to droop and drop like some of the other fatter-headed varieties. Pack the bulbs tightly into containers in early winter alongside wallflowers and some dark green foliage to offset the dazzle. Height & spread: 60cm x 20cm (24in x 8in).

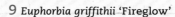

9 *Euphorbia griffithii* **'Fireglow'** (spurge) is an orange euphorbia with the same eye-catching intensity as its zingy lime-green siblings. It will add height, structure and permanence to this planting scheme as it is a hardy, long-lived shade-tolerant perennial. Its flowers are also good for picking, but watch the sap, which causes skin to blister. Height & spread: 75cm (30in).

MINIATURE GREENHOUSE

YOU WILL NEED

- miniature greenhouse (*see p.186 for suppliers*)
- gravel
- multi-purpose compost
- 2 gazania plants
- 1-2 strawberry plants
- stone chippings

One of my earliest gardening memories is spending time in my grandmother's greenhouse. Although I can't recall exactly what she grew, the scent of damp earth and the colour of the foliage, fruit and flowers have stayed with me. Here, I have recreated in miniature that romantic sensory experience.

For many people, greenhouses have a special appeal, with their hot-house micro-climate providing the perfect place for horticultural magic to happen.

In a small city plot, a full-sized, stand-alone greenhouse is something of a dream for many gardeners, but with this scaled-down version you can achieve a similar effect. The planting space, which comprises a porous concrete base, will take about three or four small plants, allowing them some room to spread. The most important consideration, however, must be the final height of your chosen plants, which will be limited by the glass roof.

I have selected some gazanias - South African natives, which are available in a range of bright shades, including vibrant reds, oranges, yellows and pinks. These daisy-like flowers love the warmth and will bloom well inside their little house, even when the sun is not shining. They grow to no more than 20cm (8in) in height, so will not be restricted by the roof. The 'Kiss Mahogany' variety I have chosen is a deep dark red with an orange centre that works beautifully with my strawberry plants, the fruits of which ripen quickly undercover and are also protected from the birds.

1. **Add a 1cm (½in) layer** of gravel over the concrete base to provide some drainage. Then fill with fresh compost to just below the rim of the container.

2. **Remove a gazania** from its polystyrene tray or pot, tease out the roots and trim off any dead, damaged or overly long leaves. Plant two or three, spacing them out equally.

3. **Remove the strawberry** plant from its pot and shake off any excess soil. Plant it between the gazanias, and firm the compost gently.

4. **Dress the compost** with stone chippings to set off the plants. Water with a small can fitted with a rose head, taking care not to wet the leaves. Put on the cover and admire.

STEAMY WINDOWS
Water the plants sparingly so that the compost is damp but never waterlogged. On hot days, if the inside starts to steam up, adjust the cover so that some air can get in, then close it up again at night.

GREEN & YELLOW

Cool greens and pale yellows combine to produce a fresh, calming scheme. Look for plants with flowers and foliage that offers textural interest too.

1 *Tulipa* **'Fringed Elegance'** is a tall variety with fringed buttercup yellow blooms that no spring garden should be without. It flowers towards the end of the season, and looks great with yellow wallflowers in a pot on a sunny patio. Height & spread: 60cm x 20cm (24in x 8in).

2 & 3 **Euphorbias** (spurge) are fantastic as foliage plants – both as a foil for the flowers in your garden and also for cutting and using in vases. Wear gloves when planting or picking any euphorbia, as they produce a white sap that irritates the skin. Try *Euphorbia amygdaloides* **var** *robbiae*, which grows well in shade – the zingy lime green bracts will brighten up any dark corner. Height & spread: 70cm x 40cm (28in x 40in). *Euphorbia cyparissias* **'Fens Ruby'** is another good variety for borders or pots, but this type prefers sun.

It is slighter shorter and works well with posy-type arrangements. Height & spread: 40cm (16in).

4 *Epimedium* **'Amber Queen'** brings a touch of light and air to the spring garden. The star-shaped flowers sit above heart-shaped leaves on delicate wiry stems. These shade-tolerant plants are ideal planted under tall shrubs and small trees, and also for indoor displays. Height & spread: 40cm x 60cm (16in x 24in).

5 *Rosa* **'Graham Thomas'** is an early flowering, award-winning golden yellow rose that is ideal for a sunny spot and moist but free-draining soil. It is available both in shrub form and as a climber – the cup-shaped flowers on both are strongly perfumed and reminiscent of violets. Height & spread: 2m (7ft).

6 **Briza maxima** (greater quaking grass) is the perfect grass for a small space. It flowers in early summer, producing little water-drop-like heads that are fabulous for drying. It also self-seeds profusely. Sow it in a sunny site and free-draining soil. Height & spread: 30cm x 10cm (12in x 4in).

7 **Erysimum 'Primrose Dame'** (wallflower) has flower heads that range from a soft pale lemon to a deep buttery yellow, and they also carry a delightful spicy scent. Grow it in sunny borders and pots; plant bare-root wallflowers the previous autumn. Height & spread: 45cm x 15cm (18in x 6in).

8 **Anethum graveolens** (dill) bears stylish clusters of bright yellow flower heads on tall straight stems. The flowers are edible, or leave them on the stems to dry out and collect the seeds for flavouring all manner of savoury dishes. A hardy annual, sow it in sun and free-draining soil. Height & spread: 90cm (36in).

9 **Bupleurum rotundifolium 'Griffithii'** is a great foliage plant for dry soil and a sunny site, with citrus green flowers and round foliage. Height & spread: 60cm x 25cm (24in x 10in).

HERB WALL

I love including homegrown herbs in my cooking all year round, and plant my own at the beginning of spring to keep me going until the first frosts, at which point I cut sprigs to dry or freeze for use in winter.

YOU WILL NEED
- 3 wall planters (*see p.186 for suppliers*)
- selection of herbs, such as lemon thyme, golden marjoram and pineapple mint
- pencil
- hammer
- 6 x sturdy plastic-coated or galvanised hooks or masonry nails
- multi-purpose compost
- small watering can

In this project I have planted up a selection of supermarket herbs. They never seem to last long if left in their original pots and packaging, but by replanting them in some fresh compost and watering them regularly you can extend their lives significantly. You can also buy herb plants from the garden centre, where you will find more varieties on offer. This quick, simple project is inexpensive to create and very easy to maintain – watering the herbs daily is the main requirement, although you can also add some fertiliser for leafy crops if the plants' foliage starts to look pale in colour or lacklustre.

There is a range of wall planters available, specifically designed for growing small plants against a vertical surface. These decorative pockets are made from durable plastic with holes at the top to hang them up, and drainage holes to prevent the plant roots from rotting. They can also be cleaned, dried and stored when not in use in winter. Each pocket is the perfect size for one standard-sized herb plant. It might be tempting to stuff a couple of herbs into each pocket, but they will not thrive if their roots are too restricted.

Selecting herbs for pockets
I have chosen a selection of herbs that look attractive when grouped together and provide flavourings for a variety of sweet and savoury dishes. Lemon thyme (*Thymus citriodorus* 'Variegatus') has tiny green and gold variegated leaves and is delicious with roast chicken. The stems of golden marjoram (*Origanum vulgare* 'Aureum') will spill over the sides of the pocket and its pickings bring a tomato salad to life. Pineapple mint (*Mentha suaveolens* 'Variegata'), which I pick for summer drinks and sorbets, has frilly green leaves dotted with cream-coloured flecks, and its fresh fruity scent will waft on the air whenever anyone brushes against it.

1. **Position your planting** pocket on a vertical surface that receives sun for at least half the day. To fix it to a wooden fence or a door, use a pencil to mark the position of the holes and then make small indentations at those points with a hammer.

2. **Screw sturdy hooks** designed for outdoor use into the indentations, ensuring they are secure. If you are positioning the planting pocket against a brick wall, simply hammer in large masonry nails. Fit the pocket onto the hooks.

3. **Add two or more** pockets underneath the first, positioning them so they slightly overlap and there are no obvious joins. Once you have all three in place, fill each one with fresh multi-purpose compost.

4. **Remove each herb** from its packaging and plant them directly into the compost, topping up with more compost if necessary. Firm down so that each is securely planted, and water well.

PURE WHITE

Elegant and eye-catching, group these blooms together with green foliage plants for a sophisticated scheme or use them as spotlights in more colourful combinations.

1 *Rosa* '**Albéric Barbier**' is a rambling rose that will reward you in many ways. Its long stems of ruffled white flowers will cover a sunny wall, but it is easy to contain in a small space if you prune it back hard after flowering. Deliciously scented, the flowers hold up well in a vase. Height & spread: up to 7m x 4m (22ft x 13ft).

2 *Ammi majus* (bishop's flower) is an annual, hugely popular among garden designers and flower arrangers and prized for its clouds of fluffy cream florets – similar to cow parsley. Sow from seed in the autumn directly in the ground or in pots in sun for early summer flowers. Height & spread: 75cm x 10cm (30in x 4in).

3 *Gaura lindheimeri* '**Whirling Butterflies**' is a long-lasting perennial that forms a hazy drift of dainty flowers that look like butterflies. Plant it on the edges of sunny beds or in pots and it will produce a show for many weeks. Height & spread: 75cm x 45cm (30in x 18in).

4 *Lobularia maritima* 'Carpet of Snow' (sweet alyssum) is one of the many varieties of this useful bedding plant that flowers all summer long. It is a hardy, low growing, wide spreading annual which works brilliantly in shallow pots and containers, and looks good combined with alpines and other miniature plants on a sunny table top. Height & spread: 10cm x 25cm (4in x 10in).

5 *Libertia chilensis* flowers reliably every year, producing pure white flower spikes that rise above sword-shaped leaves. The spikes form attractive seedheads that are good for drying. Height & spread: 90cm x 60cm (36in x 24in).

6 *Gypsophila paniculata* (baby's breath) is another favourite among the flower-arranging fraternity. A short-lived perennial, it produces airy froths of tiny flowers on virtually leafless stems. This pretty plant needs sun and free-draining soil to thrive, and it looks fantastic arranged in a big single bunch. It also dries out well. Height & spread: 50cm x 10cm (20in x 4in).

7 *Choisya ternata* (Mexican orange blossom) is a useful evergreen shrub that will grow well in sun or part shade in a small garden, or restrict its size in a container. You can prune it to shape after it has flowered in late spring, when it bears clusters of white star-shaped blooms. Its dark green foliage also has a distinctive aromatic scent. Height & spread: 2.5m (8ft).

8 *Polygonatum x hybridum* (Solomon's seal) is one of the best white-flowering perennial plants for shade. Its dainty teardrop flowers dangle from graceful arching stems, and it looks good mixed with ferns in a gloomy corner. Grow it in any soil, apart from waterlogged. Height & spread: 80cm x 40cm (32in x 16in).

9 *Bacopa* 'Snowtopia' is a dainty half-hardy trailing annual, perfect for pots and table centre-pieces in sun or part shade. Its green leafy stems are dotted with pretty little white flowers. Height & spread: 10cm x 20cm (4in x 8in).

10 *Chamaemelum nobile* (chamomile) is incredibly easy to grow from seed and has both medicinal and decorative uses. Sow it directly in the ground or in pots in a sunny spot and free-draining soil in the autumn and you will have flowers by late spring. Pick the daisy-like flowers for drying to make a calming infusion or potpourri. Height & spread: 30m x 40cm (12in x 16in).

DAISY TRIO

These joyful little plants bring back fond childhood memories of making daisy chains with my sisters on sunny summer days. You can recreate tiny fields of daisies in any small space with a few hanging planters and the self-sown plants you have at your disposal.

YOU WILL NEED

- rooted sections of Mexican daisies (*Erigeron karvinskianus*)
- soil-based compost, such as John Innes No 1, mixed with horticultural grit.
- 3 hanging planters
- drill, if needed
- dwarf marguerites
- gravel mulch (optional)

Mexican daisies (*Erigeron karvinskianus*) are ideal for this project. These happy-go-lucky daisy-like plants self-seed and grow in cracks and crevices all over the place. They flower for at least six months in my city garden, and in a protected site will bloom almost all year round. They are not fussy about their conditions and thrive in sun or part shade, although free-draining soils suit them best. They look lovely tumbling over the edges of pots and containers, and one plant will offer up several rooted babies – I even find them growing in the gaps in pavements.

1. **Mexican daisies** are easy to divide up from a parent plant, as each section has a tiny separate root system. Water the parent plant well, then use a small fork or trowel to dig up a section with roots.

2. **Pop the rooted** sections in gritty compost and keep them well watered and warm. They will soon put on some growth and start to bush out. At this point choose a hanging pot for their permanent home.

3. **Drill holes** in the bottom for drainage, using an electric hand drill, if your planter does not already have any. This set of three white tin planters come with detachable handles for balcony displays.

4. **Add a layer** of gravel or grit to the bottom of the planter to further aid drainage (these plants will not tolerate waterlogging). Fill with compost to 2cm (½in) from the rim. Then plant your new daisies.

5. **Hang the planters** from a balcony rail or the top of fence or wall, ideally in full sun or light shade. Water the plants only when the top of the compost feels dry. Snip off faded flowers to encourage more to form.

6. **Either plant more** Mexican daisies, if you have enough, or buy dwarf marguerites to fill the two adjacent planters to complete your daisy trio. This little scheme will emit sunny cheer all summer.

EXPERT TIP
Mexican daisies will overwinter in their containers as long as they don't dry out. Clip off their old flower stems too. Marguerites will not survive the winter unless they are protected from frost. Remove them and replace with more baby Mexican daisies taken from the parent plants in the spring.

PURPLE & BLUE

The soothing tones of a blue and purple palette work well with pale pinks and yellows to produce a pastel medley. A few spots of white will add highlights to the mix.

1 *Myosotis sylvatica* (forget-me-not) bridges the gap between late spring and early summer with it lacy clusters of azure blooms. Very promiscuous, it will appear in any gaps and cracks wherever the seeds can find a foothold, and grows in sun or part shade. Height & spread: 30cm x 15cm (12in x 6in).

2 *Brunnera macrophylla* 'Jack Frost' is the grown-up, elegant alternative to the forget-me-not and a plant much favoured by garden designers. It bears similar small blue flowers but is most prized for its large heart-shaped foliage, which looks like it is covered in silver frost. It makes great ground cover for shady sites. Height & spread: 40cm x 50cm (16in x 20in).

3 *Erysimum* 'Bowles's Mauve' (perennial wallflower) produces spires of deep mauve flowers that bloom from spring to late summer, providing a continuous display. Ideal for low-maintenance gardens, it prefers full sun and well-drained soil. Height & spread: 75cm x 60cm (30in x 24in).

4 *Vinca minor* (lesser periwinkle) is a great choice for a shady space, and grows well in the dry soil under trees and shrubs. Deep violet flowers appear on long trailing shoots covered with dark evergreen leaves. Easily trained upwards, it is good for vertical planting, as well as providing almost instant ground cover. Height & spread: 15cm x 50cm (6in x 20in).

5 *Iris xiphium* (Spanish iris) has deep blue or violet flowers with flashes of gold. Plant the bulbs in autumn in sun and free-draining soil. Also try Dutch irises which are very similar. Height & spread: 50cm x 10cm (20in x 4in).

6 *Nigella damascena* (love-in-a-mist) is an easy-to-grow flowering annual that will give a first-time gardener masses of confidence. Its dramatic seedpods are just as lovely as its beautiful blue flower heads, so do not cut it back. Height & spread: 45cmx 30cm (18in x 12in).

7 *Pulmonaria* **'Blue Ensign'** (lungwort) grows happily in dark shady places, its deep blue flowers and mottled green leaves lightening up any difficult corner. Height & spread: 35cm x 30cm (15in x 12in).

8 *Hyacinthoides non-scripta* (English bluebell) is a native to the English countryside, and the deep blue drifts found in woodlands in late spring offer a life-affirming picture. Use it in small beds and pots; plant the bulbs in autumn or buy plants in spring. Height & spread: 60cm x 40cm (24in x 16in).

9 *Viola odorata* (sweet violet) makes a lovely edible treat when the flowers are crystallised. The blooms are also good for creating tiny scented posies for the home. Grow it in wide shallow bowls for tabletop displays. Height & spread: 15cm x 30cm (6in x 12in).

10 *Allium cristophii* (star of Persia) is a showstopping bulb with huge spherical flower heads made up of tiny violet star-shaped blooms. Shorter than many of the ornamental alliums, plant the bulbs in autumn in full sun in a pot or the front of a sunny border in well-drained soil. The seedheads are beautiful too. Height & spread: 50cm x 20cm (20in x 8in).

DRESSED-UP DRAINPIPES

This easy-to-follow project shows how you can create a flower garden almost anywhere. I have a very unattractive drainpipe in the corner of my garden but with a little ingenuity I have made even this unpromising area into a decorative feature.

YOU WILL NEED

- plastic pots designed for a drainpipe
- gravel
- multi-purpose compost
- *Lithodora* plants
- *Lobelia* plants
- watering can or jug
- high potash fertiliser

One easy way to disguise a boring drainpipe is with purpose-designed plastic pots, which come with ready-made drainage holes and a strap that allows you to fix them firmly onto a drain- or down-pipe. They are extremely durable and will provide a home for plants for many seasons.

My plants are limited to two varieties. *Lithodora diffusa* 'Grace Ward' is a low-growing, mat-forming perennial that bears azure star-shaped flowers from late spring to early autumn. It hints at the promise of bright blue skies to come when it first appears. Its hairy leaves mean that it is good at retaining water but, as with plants in any small container, it will need watering daily or twice daily in spring and summer.

I interspersed the *Lithodora* with lobelia bedding plants, the kind that you see in hanging baskets, which are perfect for this project. Available in trays of plug plants from the garden centre in late spring, these blooms are tender so do not plant them outside until all risk of frost has passed. I used a lilac variety to complement the blue *Lithodora*. Lobelia dies back in autumn and can be replaced with violas or cyclamen to extend the interest at this time of year.

1. **The drainpipe pots** have a removable base and a strap to fix them to the pipe. Detach the base to reveal the drainage holes first.

4. **Plant the *Lithodora*** in your drainpipe pot, and fill any gaps in between with the lobelia plug plants. Firm the compost down gently to remove any air gaps.

EXPERT TIP
I have painted the brick wall behind the pots black to disguise the drainpipe further. If the pots dry out and the flowers start to wilt, remove from the drainpipe and place them in a bucket of water for a day to rehydrate.

2. **Add gravel** to the base of the pot for added drainage. Then fill almost to the top with a multi-purpose compost enriched with fertilisers.

3. **Attach the pot** to your drainpipe at the desired height and check it is firmly fixed in position. Repeat steps 1-3 for the other pots.

5. **Plant up the remaining** containers with the rest of the plants. I have used the same combination of plants in each pot to produce this simple, coordinated display.

6. **Water the pots** gently every day, and feed the plants regularly with a high potash fertiliser after a few weeks, when the food in the compost is exhausted.

BURGUNDY & PINK

Summer containers and borders will be enriched with a palette of soft pinks and rich burgundies. Also look out for bedding plants in matching colours to fill gaps.

1 & 2 *Astrantia major* **'Ruby Star'** (masterwort) is a traditional cottage-garden plant, but it has been appearing more and more in contemporary planting schemes. The flowers, with their tight pincushion heads, bloom for ages and the plant copes well with part shade. Try weaving this deep claret-coloured variety with the pale pink **A.** *major* **'Florence'**. Height & spread: 45cm x 50cm (18in x 20in).

3 *Cosmos bipinnatus* **'Fizzy Pink'** is just one of these pretty sun-loving plants that I have recommended for summer palettes. They are incredibly easy to grow from seed, either directly in a pot or a narrow border, and they flower prolifically so you have plenty to pick without denuding the plant. Height & spread: 60cm x 30cm (24in x 12in).

4 *Monarda* **'Neon'** (pink bergamot), like all bergamots, is a bee magnet. Its pale pink fringed flower heads create dense nectar-rich clusters above highly aromatic foliage. Plants prefer moist soil and sun or part shade. Height & spread: 80cm x 45cm (32in x 18in).

5 *Rosa* **'Blush Noisette'** is a repeat-flowering rambling rose that grows well in a sunny or partly shaded small space. Leave it to push up through other shrubs rather than training it against a wall or fence. The pompom flowers are highly scented and keep coming in generous quantities. Height & spread: 3m x 75cm (10ft x 30in).

6 *Geranium sanguineum* **var.** *striatum* (cranesbill) has pretty pale pink flowers with delicate darker streaks. It will spread quite rapidly and makes excellent ground cover in sun or shade. Divide clumps to make new plants in autumn or spring. Height & spread: 40cm x 50cm (16in x 20in).

7 *Daucus carota* 'Dara' (wild carrot) often appears in naturalistic schemes but looks good in more formal designs too. The flowers are like pink clouds and bring light and air into a sunny urban space. It prefers moist soil. Height & spread: 80cm x 40cm (32in x 16in).

8 *Sanguisorba officinalis* (burnet) is a favourite plant for naturalistic schemes. The unusual small bead-like flower heads, which are held on slim wiry stems, are an intense claret and hold their colour well once picked and dried. They also last for ages in a vase without any water. Plant it in sun or part shade and well-drained soil. Height & spread: 1.2m x 60cm (4ft x 2ft).

9 *Echinacea purpurea* (cone flower) is a must for a summer scheme, and after its petals have faded you can pick them off to retain the inner cone-shaped seedheads on the stems through autumn and winter. It prefers full sun and any soil that isn't too dry. Height & spread: 60cm x 20cm (24in x 8in).

RAMBLING ROSE TEPEE

Having a tiny space doesn't mean that you can't grow roses. Some varieties are quite happy in large pots and containers, including compact climbers such as this pretty pale pink variety.

YOU WILL NEED

- 3 bamboo canes 1.5m (5ft) in length
- paintbrush and exterior wood paint in a shade matching the rose
- large container, at least 50cm (20in) deep and wide
- vermiculite
- horticultural grit
- soil-based compost, e.g. John Innes No 3
- Little Rambler rose or a short climbing rose
- twine and thin wire
- scissors or secateurs
- pinks and *Daucus carota*

In this project I have used a small rambler to create a tepee of total deliciousness. The variety is Little Rambler, and its tiny, pale pink pompom flowers have a gorgeous scent. The hips look pretty in winter too.

I chose a pot measuring 50cm (20in) deep by 50cm (20in) in diameter. Roses need width more than depth and will only complain if they can't spread their roots. The pot is made from lightweight plastic, so even when it is planted I can move it around quite easily.

1. **Paint three bamboo** canes of the same length – I have used 1.5m (5ft) lengths – using exterior wood paint in a shade that will match your rose. Leave them to dry thoroughly. Apply a second coat if needed.

2. **Check that your pot** has drainage holes in the bottom and drill a few if necessary. Then add a layer of horticultural grit and vermiculite to the base of the pot, so it is about a quarter full, and top up with compost.

3. **Plant the rose** in the hole. I am planting to one side of the pot because I want to add some smaller plants at the front, but you could set it in the centre if just planting the rose. Firm around the roots to remove air gaps.

4. **Insert the painted** canes at equal intervals around the edge of the container, taking care not to damage the rose's rootball. Fasten them securely at the top with coloured twine to match the canes and rose.

5. **The rose has a new** framework to ramble over, but first remove the old support to which the stems were originally tied in their original pot. Carefully snip off the plastic bindings and slide out the old canes.

6. **Firm the compost** around the holes left by the old canes. Now tie the rose onto its new support by wiring on the tallest stems, or tying them on with twine. Do not tie them too tightly or you may damage the stems.

7. **Underplant the roses** with some perfumed pinks (*Dianthus*) to blend with their scent, and add a few Queen Anne's lace (*Daucus carota* 'Dara') seedlings for a hint of hedgerow wildness. Water in the plants well.

8. **Water the rose pot** and tie in the stems regularly. Remove the faded blooms but leave them in autumn if you want hips. In spring, dig out a little compost and add fresh compost, and granular rose fertiliser.

ORANGE & RED

Fiery shades of red and orange are illuminated further under the blaze of the midsummer sun. Use them to draw the eye to a border or container display on a patio.

1 *Achillea* **'Terracotta'** (yarrow) has flat-topped flower heads made up of clusters of tiny florets. These fantastic flowers are ideal for cutting and last well in a vase. Plant yarrows in full sun and well-drained soil. Height & spread: 80cm x 40cm (32in x 16in).

2 *Helenium* **'Moerheim Beauty'** (sneezeweed) has rich red daisy-like flowers that attract bees and butterflies. Plant it in full sun and moist, free-draining soil. Height & spread: 90cm x 60cm (36in x 24in).

3 *Rudbeckia hirta* **'Cherry Brandy'** (black-eyed Susan) produces large daisy-like flowers in shades of carmine that bloom from summer to autumn. It is a good pollinator plant and the birds will feast on the seedheads over winter. Plant it in sun or part shade and soil that does not dry out. Height & spread: 60cm x 40cm (24in x 16in).

5

6

7

8

9

4 & 5 *Echinacea* **'Irresistible'** and **'Tomato Soup'** (coneflower) are both joyous beauties and well worth growing for their rich orange flowers. They prefer to be in full sun and fertile soil. The root extract of *Echinacea* is a well-known herbal remedy for preventing colds. Height & spread: 70cm x 30cm (27in x 12in).

6 *Antirrhinum majus* **'Scarlet'** (snapdragon) is a deep red form of this popular annual bedding plant. It is a great flower for cutting, and you can grow it easily from seed – it will then self-sow profusely. Grow it in full sun and moist but well-drained soil. Height & spread: 60cm x 20cm (24in x 8in).

7 *Zinnia elegans* **'Orange King'**, like all zinnias, will grow well in a pot and makes a wonderful cut flower. You will find several varieties in similar shades for a fiery colour scheme, or combine it with the *Echinacea* and *Helenium* from this palette for a hot sunny floral mix. Grow it in full sun and free-draining soil. Height & spread: 60cm x 30cm (24in x 12in).

8 *Papaver cambricum* (Welsh poppy) flowers continously all summer long. It will grow in dappled shade and will light up a difficult corner. Grow it from seed or buy young plants in spring; it will then self-seed to decorate all areas of your garden. Height & spread: 50cm x 40cm (20in x 16in).

9 *Rosa* **Lady of Shalott** is a dusky orange rose with deliciously fragrant flowers that smell like spiced apples and cloves. Ideal for cutting, this disease-resistant variety blooms continuously throughout the summer. Plant it in sun or light shade and moisture-retentive soil. Height & spread: 1.2m x 90cm (4ft x 3ft).

ORANGE CLIMBING NASTURTIUMS

YOU WILL NEED

- exterior paint for plastic surfaces
- piece of guttering
- small decorative piece of trellis
- garden soil or multi-purpose compost
- nasturtium seeds
- seed tray and seed compost (optional)
- vermiculite
- watering can

Very easy to grow, nasturtiums have many benefits for the city gardener. Their dazzling flowers will brighten up any small garden or patio pot, and both the blooms and foliage are edible, their sharp peppery flavour jazzing up a plain green salad and other cold dishes.

If you have next to no outdoor space, nasturtiums will be your best unfussy friend. There is a good reason why these pretty flowers are commonly seen in primary school gardening schemes – they are incredibly simple to grow and prefer poor, dry soil. Their only other requirement is some sun. Here I am growing them in some guttering that I found in the street. I cut it to size with a hacksaw to match an attractive rusted trellis, which provides the plants with a frame to climb. If you do not have trellis or the wall space, plant in a pot with a bamboo-cane wigwam support (*see p.129*).

1. **Paint the guttering** with non-toxic exterior paint suitable for plastics in a shade to match the wall. Leave to dry and apply a second coat if necessary. This creates a seamless, coordinated effect, which I prefer.

2. **I raised these** nasturtium flowers from seed in a tray. To do this, sow into good quality seed compost and place in a sheltered spot until germinated. Alternatively, sow where you want them to grow.

3. **Fill the guttering** to the top with garden soil that has some grit in it, or multi-purpose compost. You may need to add a large stone or plastic at either end of the guttering to prevent the soil falling out.

4. **Transplant your** seedlings into the guttering, setting them 10cm (4in) apart. If you sow them directly into the gutter, space the seeds 5cm (2in) apart, and thin them if they all germinate to 10cm (4in).

6. **After a few weeks**, the plants should have put on good growth and will start to flower. Deadhead faded flowers, or use them in full bloom for salads or as a garnish. Removing the flowers regularly encourages more blooms to form.

5. **Once planted**, cover the seedlings with a layer of vermiculite, which will help to retain moisture around them. Water them every day or two, even during rainy weather, as the area directly next to a wall or fence will remain dry.

EXPERT TIP
Young nasturtium seedlings are a favourite target for slugs and snails. I like to garden organically and as I eat the flowers and leaves, I don't spray them or put down slug pellets. I keep these pests at bay by putting used coffee grounds around my plants; the caffeine and gritty texture is believed to act as a deterrent.

High summer palette

YELLOW & GREEN

Cool down a summer scheme with calming greens and buttery yellows, with just a few sparks of bright gold to inject some drama into this muted colour scheme.

1 *Alchemilla mollis* (lady's mantle) is near the top of every flower arranger's list. Its frothy, lime green flowers make perfect fillers and last well in a vase. In a border, its scallop-shaped leaves catch water droplets so they glisten and sparkle. It is happy in sun or shade and any soil. Height & spread: 40cm x 75cm (16in x 30in).

2 *Zinnia* **'Benary's Giant Lime'** has totally green flowers, which makes it an unusual plant to grow, either from seed or from seedlings bought in early summer for flowers later in the season. It likes a spot in full sun and free-draining soil. Height & spread: 40cm x 30cm (16in x 12in).

3 *Echinacea purpurea* **'Green Jewel'** (coneflower) is best suited to a hot spot, either in a border or in a large container. If you give it enough sun it will flower through until the first frosts. Height & spread: 50cm x 30cm (20in x 12in).

4 *Cosmos bipinnatus* **'Xanthos'** has pale lemon daisy-like blooms and slots beautifully into a yellow-green scheme. Easy to grow from seed, it will flower all summer long. Height & spread: 50cm x 30cm (20in x 12in).

5 *Achillea* **'Moonshine'** (yarrow) is a bright yellow variety and grows more vigorously than some other forms. If you have space for a dedicated cutting patch, it is also great for picking. Grow it in full sun and free-draining soil. Height & spread: 50cm x 30cm (20in x 12in).

6 *Anthemis tinctoria* (dyer's chamomile) has bright yellow daisies which were traditionally used to colour fabric. Grow this clump-forming perennial in sun and free-draining soil for flowers year after year. Height & spread: 50cm (20in).

7 *Hemerocallis citrina* (daylily) is a pale yellow variety with lightly scented flowers. Each bloom lasts for one day only, hence its common name, but because they arrive in a steady stream all summer, it still provides a great show. Grow this plant in sun or part shade and fertile soil. Height & spread: 1.2m x 75cm (4ft x 30in).

8 *Hakonechloa macra* **'Aureola'** is a small ornamental grass that grows to form a rounded hummock of deciduous leaves. It bears arching stems of lime green flower in high summer and the foliage is a great filler in vases. It prefers sun or part shade and moist soil. Height & spread: 35cm x 40cm (15in x 16in).

9 *Hydrangea arborescens* **'Lime Rickey'** produces large, lime green flower heads continuously throughout the summer, lending a lovely freshness to any surrounding planting scheme. Leave the heads to dry off on their stems and bring them indoors for a winter arrangement. Cut back in the spring to keep it compact in a small space. Height & spread: 1.2m (4ft).

UPCYCLED TIN CAN DISPLAY

YOU WILL NEED
- tobacco plant seeds
- seed tray
- seed compost
- a variety of large fruit or vegetable cans
- hammer and nail
- multi-purpose compost
- cosmos and coneflower seedlings (optional)
- small watering can

The stars of this project are the annual lime green tobaccco plants (*Nicotiana*), which I grew from seed in early spring and combined with cosmos and coneflowers to produce this pretty yet inexpensive display in upcycled tin cans.

The lime green hue of this variety of tobacco plant is quite stunning. It looks great in a display all by itself but to highlight its beauty I have displayed it with a tin of pale yellow cosmos and lime green coneflowers (*Echinacea purpurea* 'Green Jewel' - *see p.134*), together with cut sprigs of *Bupleurum* (*see p.115*), to complete the lime zest picture.

An inexpensive way to display plants, tin cans provide good homes for annuals, which do not have large roots systems. For tips on sowing half-hardy annuals indoors, *see pp.84–85*.

1. Look out for large tin cans – catering sizes are ideal and you may be able to pick them up free from a local cafe or restaurant. Make drainage holes in the bottom of each tin with a hammer and nail.

2. Fill a large can almost to the top with multi-purpose compost. Gently transplant four or five seedlings into the can using a teaspoon to scoop out the roots. To avoid any damage, handle the seedlings with care.

3. As the seedlings become established, take out all but the strongest healthiest plant to give it space to flourish and flower. If the others are growing well too, pop them in their own tin can filled with compost.

4. It took five months from sowing to flowering, so patience is the name of the game. Water the tins every day or two, and remove faded blooms to encourage more to form. You can also harvest the seed in autumn (*see p.180*).

WHITE & CREAM

Use these plants between those suggested for early summer to keep the show going until the first frosts. The hydrangea's seed heads sustain interest in winter too.

1 *Orlaya grandiflora* (white laceflower) is a graceful umbellifer, with flat heads made up of tiny individual flowers which look like lace. Grow it in full sun and free-draining soil. Height & spread: 45cm x 30cm (18in x 12in).

2 *Hydrangea paniculata* 'Grandiflora' is a deciduous shrub that bears large clusters of cone-shaped flowers in late summer. You can grow it in a large pot on its own or plant it in the middle of a sunny or partly shaded border for some shape and structure. Dry the flowers and bring them indoors. Height & spread: 3m x 2m (10ft x 7ft).

3 *Anemone x hybrida* 'Honorine Jobert' (Japanese anemone) is a beautiful mid- to late-summer flowering perennial with clear white blooms. Plant it in any soil, except waterlogged, and a sunny or partly shaded spot, and a small clump will soon increase in size. Height & spread: 90cm (36in).

4 *Rosa* **'Madame Alfred Carrière'** will climb up even a north-facing wall or fence, decorating it with creamy white double flowers with an intoxicating scent. Prune it hard in late winter to contain it in a small space. Height & spread: 6m x 3m (20ft x 10ft).

5 *Cosmos bipinnatus* **'Purity'** makes a great value cut flower. Sow the seeds in batches from late spring and it will still be flowering for picking up to the first frosts. Grow plants in sun and free-draining soil. Height & spread: 1.2m x 60cm (4ft x 24in).

6 *Verbena* **Vepita 'White'** is an annual, perfect for growing in pots and containers. It has a compact habit and will flower continuously all summer, given sun and moist compost. Height & spread: 20cm (8in).

7 *Dianthus chinensis* (Chinese pink) is an old-fashioned cottage garden plant that adapts well to a small urban space. It carries the most divine perfume. Grow it in pots or a border in sun and free-draining soil. Height & spread: 20cm x 30cm (8in x 12in).

8 *Matthiola incana alba* (stock) is a perfumed white stock, used widely in cottage-garden schemes, although it also suits modern gardens. Its flowers sit atop lush foliage and it needs sun and moist but free-draining soil. Height & spread: 50cm x 30cm (20in x 12in).

9 *Antirrhinum* **'White Giant'** (snapdragon) is an extra tall variety, great for layering – the tall flower spikes tower majestically over shorter plants in a sunny border. Height & spread: 90cm x 30cm (36in x 12in).

10 *Leucanthemum vulgare* (ox-eye daisy) brings echoes of the countryside to the city. These daisies will multiply quickly in full sun and free-draining soil, providing lots of cutting material for natural, loose-shaped posies and jam jar arrangements. Height & spread: 60cm (24in).

WHITE SUSPENDED GERANIUMS

Gardening in the air is the perfect way of making use of the vertical space in a tiny garden, and drought-tolerant geraniums (*Pelargonium*) are the perfect plants to suspend in these innovative pots.

YOU WILL NEED

- hanging planters (*see p.186 for suppliers*)
- multi-purpose compost and grit
- 3 white geraniums
- small watering can
- sturdy hooks for suspending the pots

This project uses hanging planters, which are widely available online and in garden centres, but the trick is to find lightweight types that will hang from a single hook without the whole display crashing to the ground.

I have planted them with the single white geranium *Pelargonium* 'Toscana Wenke' which is known for is upright growing habit. Although I am turning it on its head, the planters look best with individual straight-growing plants. They need something that requires little watering, so these bedding geraniums or any other type of drought-loving Mediterranean plant fit the bill too. White lavenders, for example, would look equally fabulous.

1. **Buy pots specially** designed for upside down displays. They will include a sponge which you soak in water before fitting it into the bottom of the container.

2. **Fill the pot** almost to the rim with some multi-purpose compost mixed with horticultural grit or gravel. Water the plants now and set to one side to drain.

3. **Fold the mesh fabric** provided in half and cut a hole in the centre to fit around the geranium stems. This will hold the plant in place when it is suspended upside down.

4. **Slip the mesh** over the leafy stems, taking care not to damage them. It should fit quite snugly, preventing any compost around the roots of the plant from falling out.

5. **Tidy the geranium** plants by removing any dead or yellowing leaves and brown flowers. You can also trim the roots a little if they do not fit comfortably in the container, then plant it.

6. **Gently firm** the compost around the roots to remove any air gaps. Screw the lid on the planter, taking care not to damage the foliage or flowers. Repeat steps 1-6 for the other plants.

7. **Insert the metal** eyes provided into each of the pots. Attach the wire hooks to the eyes, or use some strong twine or ribbon if you prefer, and suspend upside down from another sturdy hook.

8. **Water the plant** from the top of the pot. Fill the dish-like area carefully with water. It will then seep through the holes into the sponge below, keeping both the compost and plants' roots moist.

High summer palette

PURPLE & BLUE

These flowers are perfect for pots and borders, where their soft shades put on a show for many weeks in midsummer, with some blooming until early autumn.

1 *Geranium* **Rozanne** (cranesbill) is covered with saucer-shaped blue flowers with white eyes from early summer to early autumn. Grow it in sun or light shade and well-drained soil. Height & spread: 60cm x 80cm (24in x 32in).

2 *Agapanthus africanus* (African lily) makes a statement in this colour scheme with its bold spherical flower heads and strappy leaves. Plant it tightly in a pot, as it flowers best with restricted roots. Height & spread: 90cm x 60cm (36in x 24in).

3 *Cerinthe major* **'Purpurascens'** is one of the easiest annuals to grow from seed. Although the blooms aren't particularly dramatic, the deep purple bells

and surrounding blue bracts make it a great filler for cut flower arrangements. It loves dry soil and a sunny site, and will self-seed if conditions are right. Height & spread: 60cm x 30cm (24in x 12in).

4 *Salvia nemorosa* **'Ostfriesland'** is one of the most reliable of the perennial salvias. Its deep violet flower spikes put on a show all summer and are magnets for bees. Grow it in full sun and free-draining soil. Height & spread: 45cm x 60cm (18in x 24in).

5 *Salvia viridis* (clary sage) is an easy annual to grow from seed. Plant it in clumps, so you can pick from it freely, in sun and moist but well-drained soil. Height & spread: 45cm x 30cm (18in x 12in).

6 *Verbena rigida* is a good perennial for pots in a small sunny space, either planted on its own or as part of a mixed scheme. Cut the flowers back as they die off and more will keep coming. Height & spread: 60cm x 40cm (24in x 16in).

7 *Lavandula angustifolia* **'Hidcote'** (English lavender) is one of my favourite varieties. Grow this compact lavender in a pot or, if you have space, use several to line a sunny pathway. The scent is its most valuable quality. Pick the flowers as they fade and make your own lavender sachets (*see* p.94). Grow it in free-draining soil. Height & spread: 60cm (24in).

8 *Nepeta x faassenii* (catmint) is as effective as lavender for lining a path or edging a border. The blue flower spikes and silvery green foliage are also great for cutting. Grow it in sun and free-draining soil. Height & spread: 60cm x 45cm (24in x 18in).

9 *Delphinium* **Summer Skies Group** says it all when it comes to selecting a plant for high summer. The elegant towering spires of powder-blue flowers will bring on a holiday mood, even if you are rushing off to the office. Plant these delphiniums in as much sun as possible and moist but well-drained soil. Cut back when the flowers fade to encourage a second flush. Height & spread: 1.5m x 60cm (5ft x 2ft).

143

MORNING GLORY CLOCHE

Morning glory is just that. It is an annual plant that puts on a spectacular display of trumpet-shaped blooms, which appear at first light and fade by mid-afternoon, only to do the same thing the next day and every day after that for several months in summer.

For a lesson in transitory beauty this pretty plant is the perfect example. Enjoy the blooms while they last, but if you want to extend their lifespan, try picking them early in the morning and floating them in a glass bowl of ice-cold water.

Although it is possible to grow *Ipomoea,* or morning glory, from seed, mine failed to germinate. Unfortunately this happens from time to time for no obvious reason, however much gardening experience you have. I ended up buying a small plant of a variety called *Ipomoea tricolor* 'Heavenly Blue'.

I transferred it to a larger pot that sits happily on a portable tray within the confines of a domed wire cloche. The idea is to allow the stems to twine through and over the cloche to cover it with flowers and foliage.

YOU WILL NEED

- wire cloche and tray
- plastic pot to fit
- morning glory plant
- multi-purpose compost
- scissors and stick
- high potash fertiliser

1. **Fill the pot** to 5cm (2in) from the rim with compost, making sure that the pot fits beneath the cloche and has drainage holes in the base. Plant the morning glory in the centre, firming around it with more compost.

2. **Gently unravel** the plants' stems from their original support canes. Then carefully remove the canes, taking care not to damage the plant. Add compost to the holes left by the canes and firm with your fingers.

3. **Poke the delicate** unfurled stems through the cloche with the help of a kebab stick. Once it gets going, morning glory is quite rampant and the stems will cling to the cloche wires unaided.

4. **Set in a sunny**,
warm place and water
the plant regularly.
If you used compost
enriched with fertiliser
you should not need
to add more for a few
weeks, but then apply
a high potash fertiliser
every fortnight.

Autumn palette

ORANGE & RED

Match the fiery shades of autumn leaves with this palette of eye-catching spicy red and orange blooms, guaranteed to cut through the gloom on cool, misty days.

1, 2 & 3 Dahlias are the flowers most associated with autumn and harvest festivals. There are thousands of varieties, but for pretty pumpkin colours, try combining the cactus flower types, *Dahlia* **'Vulcan'**, **'Kenora Sunset'** and **'Doris Day'**, in pots on a sunny patio. They will bloom for many weeks and lift the spirits until the first frosts signal the arrival of winter. Height & spread: 1.2m x 40cm (4ft x 16in).

4 *Crocosmia* **'Lucifer'** (montbretia) is the boldest of all crocosmias. Its bright scarlet sprays of funnel-shaped flowers are real showstoppers in late summer and early autumn. A clump-forming perennial plant, it likes sun or part shade and free-draining soil. Divide large clumps in the spring. Height & spread: 1m x 80cm (39in x 32in).

5 *Kniphofia* (red hot poker) or torch lilies come into their own towards the end of summer and in autumn. Originally from South Africa, these perennials add height and drama with their vibrant orange-red spikes. They enjoy sun or part shade, and moist but free-draining soil. Height & spread: 1m x 60cm (39in x 24in).

6 *Cosmos atrosanguineus* **Chocamocha** (chocolate cosmos) is a perennial and, unlike the annual varieties, it will flower year after year in a pot or well-drained sunny bed. The dark maroon flower heads have a sumptuous, velvety texture and smell like chocolate. Height & spread: 45cm x 30cm (18in x 12in).

7 *Hypericum* **x** *inodorum* (St John's wort) produces yellow flowers in the summer but they really come into their own in autumn when the red or orange berries appear. They look fantastic in an indoor arrangement and are easy to preserve. Plant in sun or shade and moist but well-drained soil. Height & spread: 90cm x 60cm (36in x 24in).

8 *Agastache* 'Painted Lady' (hyssop) has pinkish blooms that turn a deep apricot as they open. A good bee plant for sun and free-draining soil, the flowers rise above aromatic foliage that smells of liquorice. Leave the flowers to dry out on their stems as food for the birds over winter. Height & spread: 90cm x 40cm (36in x 16in).

9 Chrysanthemum flowers are used around the world in the celebrations for All Saints Day or the Day of the Dead. They will keep blooming outside until winter sets in, given sun and fertile free-draining soil. Height & spread: up to 1m x 30cm (39in x 12in).

10 *Tithonia rotundifolia* 'Torch' (Mexican sunflower) is a half-hardy annual that you can grow from seed in the spring. Its deep tawny colour and luscious velvety petals combine to make a fabulous flower for picking when many others are starting to fade. Plant it in sun and free-draining soil. Height & spread: 1.2m x 45cm (4ft x 18in).

DAHLIAS IN A VINTAGE FRUIT CRATE

YOU WILL NEED
- fruit or vegetable crate
- hessian to fit crate
- dahlia tubers
- multi-purpose compost
- horticultural grit
- spade and scissors

Dahlias put on a fantastic show of blooms from late summer until the first frosts, but to create this blaze of colour you need to start them off in mid-spring. They grow from finger-like tubers and thrive in pots and containers, such as these fruit crates.

I have planted my dahlia tubers in a vintage fruit crate lined with hessian and filled with multi-purpose compost. I like the idea of using a rustic crate to display these autumn blooms as its roughly hewn finish contrasts beautifully with the showy flowers. You can find crates online but any sturdy wooden box will work equally well. The tubers started to put on some growth in late spring, a few weeks after they had been planted, and the more sun they receive the quicker they will grow and flower. In sheltered city gardens, you will not need to lift them over winter.

1. **Choose a sturdy** wooden crate – flimsy types will not be suitable, as they may rot and break when you try to lift or move them. Fill the crate to about one third full with compost.

2. **The key to success** with dahlia tubers is to ensure you plant them the right way up, with the central stem at the top and the bulbous, finger-like sections spread over the compost.

3. **Before planting,** apply a thin layer of horticultural grit under and around each group of tubers to provide extra drainage. Place the tubers on top and cover with more compost.

4. **Fill the crate** to about 5cm (2in) from the top with compost, which will allow space for watering. Then trim the hessian to the edge of the crate, and set in a sunny sheltered spot.

4. After about ten weeks I had plenty of bushy foliage and, to great excitement, tight green buds started to appear. It took another couple of weeks for the flowers to burst forth. I planted *Dahlia* 'Jescot Julie' and 'New Baby' to bring contrast in shape and form to this display. If there is space in your crate, you could also add small clumps of orange *Crocosmia* between or behind the dahlias; their tall thin spires contrast well with the rounded dahlia flower heads.

EXPERT TIP
Dahlia tubers will rot in soggy compost but they are unlikely to do so here, as the crate has gaps in the base and hessian is permeable. If you are using a different pot, ensure it has drainage holes.

PURPLE & BLUE

While hot summer sun can bleach these subtle shades, the softer light of autumn brings them into focus. Combine them with other mellow colours for a soothing mix.

1 *Symphyotrichum* **'Little Carlow'** (aster) will reliably fill a small space with colour in late autumn. It flowers prolifically, bearing clusters of lilac daisy-like heads that have a tendency to self-seed everywhere. Height & spread: 90cm x 45cm (36in x 18in).

2 *Pennisetum alopecuroides* (fountain grass) is a beautiful deciduous grass with blue-purple plumes of flowers that look fabulous swaying in the breeze. Plant it in clumps to line a sunny, well-drained border or individually in containers, and pick to bring inside for drying over the winter. Height & spread: 75cm x 50cm (30in x 20in).

3 *Liriope muscari* (blue lily-turf) is often seen in public planting schemes and for good reason. Flowering from late summer to late autumn, its dainty purple flower spikes will continue through into winter in sheltered areas, when there is little else to see. It also loves shade but needs acid soil to thrive. Height & spread: 40cm (16in).

4 *Geranium pyrenaicum* **'Bill Wallis'** (mountain cranesbill) comes from the Pyrenees, which explains its common name. Capable of withstanding cold, harsh conditions, it will continue to display its tiny mauve flowers into late autumn. Grow it in sun or part shade and well-drained soil. Height & spread: 30cm x 20cm (12in x 8in).

5 *Callicarpa bodinieri* **var.** *giraldii* **'Profusion'** (beauty berry) bears clusters of bright purple fruits, which are a hit with flowers arrangers and the cut stems can also be used for preserving. Grow it in full sun and well-drained soil. Height & spread: 3m x 2.5m (10ft x 8ft).

6 *Salvia* **'Purple Majesty'** is a very late flowering salvia. Its deep blue flowering whorls are a whole 2.5cm (1in) in length and a great attraction for any late pollinators. It thrives in sun and free-draining soil. Height & spread: 90cm x 45in (36in x 18in).

7 *Cobaea scandens* (cup and saucer vine) has fragrant cup-shaped flowers which change from greenish-white to deep purple as they mature. A vigorous annual climber, train the stems over a sunny wall or on a trellis, and grow in moist but well-drained soil. Height & spread: up to 6m (20ft).

8 *Aconitum* **'Stainless Steel'** (monk's hood) is a beautiful pale blue form of this poisonous perennial. Handle it with care and wear gloves when cutting the flowers for indoor displays. Grow it in partial shade and moist but well-drained soil. Height & spread: 90cm x 30cm (36in x 12in).

9 *Hydrangea serrata* **'Bluebird'** is a sought-after variety with blue-mauve flowers that bloom until autumn. To keep the colour true, plant in moist acid soil or ericaceous compost. Let the flowers dry out on the stem for use as winter decorations. Plants like some shade. Height & spread: 1.2m (4ft).

10 *Crocus speciosus* lifts the spirits when planted in drifts to create a carpet of dainty purple flowers. The blooms appear before the leaves, and left to their own devices, these bulbs will quickly naturalise in a sunny site. If space is tight, pot them up in gritty compost. Height & spread: 15cm x 5cm (6in x 2in).

PORTABLE PURPLE TRUG

I am not alone in choosing the elegant *Verbena bonariensis* as one of my favourite plants – speak to any garden designer and they will name it too. The tall branching stems topped with clusters of tiny purple flowers make a stylish focal point.

This tall perennial verbena is great for picking and works well at the front, middle or back of a mixed border in any sunny planting scheme. You will see it in traditional cottage gardens and set out in fashionable swathes in prairie schemes, where it is often mixed with grasses that have the same light and airy see-through quality. Here, I have planted it in a plastic trug in a matching colour and positioned it where the blooms can bask in sun.

1. **This trug does not have** drainage holes so I have made a few with an electric drill. This is important as verbena hate soggy conditions. To keep the trug as light as possible and to create more drainage, I have filled the base with 5-6 plastic pots cut in half with secateurs or scisssors.

2. **I planted about ten baby** *Verbena bonariensis* plants that had seeded themselves from a parent growing in my garden. It self-seeds profusely in gravel or free-draining soil, which is another thing I love about it – who wouldn't want plants like this for free? Buy one and you will be rewarded many times over.

3. **Plant the seedlings** in the compost, ensuring all the roots are covered. Firm them in gently. Add a layer of slate chippings on top of the compost to finish off the display. Place the trug in a sunny spot and water every few days. The plants should continue to bloom until the first frosts or beyond.

EXPERT TIP
Place the trug where it looks good, and when flowering is over, set it close to the house or other sheltered area where it will not get too wet in winter. Feed in spring with an all-purpose fertiliser.

YELLOW & GREEN

Winter and the first few weeks of spring can be dispiriting, but some evergreen foliage and bright sunny flowers can banish the blues and help you to enjoy the cold seasons.

1 & 2 *Narcissus* **'February Gold'** (daffodil) flowers in late winter and grows well in pots and window boxes, bringing much early cheer. Plant the bulbs in autumn in clumps for the best effect. Mix it with the later flowering *Narcissus* **'Jack Snipe'** for a showstopping display. Height & spread: 25cm x 10cm (10in x 4in).

3 *Helleborus foetidus* (stinking hellebore) has lovely pale green flowers that appear from mid-winter to spring. The 'stink' is only released if you crush the leaves. Grow it in shade and moist soil. Height & spread: 80cm x 45cm (32in x 18in).

4 *Eranthis hyemalis* (winter aconite) produce buttercup-like flowers in an intense sunny yellow

with bright green cuffs that shine through the gloom. In autumn, plant drifts of bulbs in moist soil and sun or shade, or pot them up in soil-based compost. Height & spread: 10cm x 5cm (4in x 2in).

5 *Polystichum setiferum* (soft shield fern) has handsome evergreen fronds that look great in any shady urban setting. Either use it as a foil for bright yellow flowers in a mixed scheme in well-drained soil, or display it in a statement pot. Height & spread: 1.2m x 90cm (4ft x 3ft).

6

6 *Euphorbia oblongata* (eggleaf spurge) flowers almost all year round in a sheltered spot. It makes a great cut flower, but beware its milky sap, which causes skin irritations. Grow it from seed sown in early spring in dappled shade and moist but free-draining soil. Height & spread: 60cm (24in).

7 *Primula vulgaris* (primrose) is a European native that grows in the wild in shady woodlands and under hedgerows in moist but well-drained soil. Its pale yellow flower heads also look good in an urban setting, taking you to another time and place. Height & spread: 20cm x 30cm (8in x 12in).

7

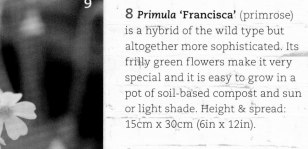

9

8

8 *Primula 'Francisca'* (primrose) is a hybrid of the wild type but altogether more sophisticated. Its frilly green flowers make it very special and it is easy to grow in a pot of soil-based compost and sun or light shade. Height & spread: 15cm x 30cm (6in x 12in).

9 *Primula veris* (cowslip) also belongs to the primrose family and is native to the British Isles. It looks beautiful in a natural or wildflower scheme, its small lemon-yellow heads standing tall above the leaves. Grow it in moist soil and sun or part shade. Height & spread: 25cm (10in).

YELLOW AND GREEN TIERED PLANTING SCHEME

YOU WILL NEED

- large decorative pot
- smaller plastic pot to fit inside it
- scissors
- soil-based compost, e.g, John Innes No 3
- *Cornus sericea* 'Flaviramea'
- *Narcissus* 'Tête-à-Tête'
- variegated lemon thyme
- natural twine (optional)
- watering can

I have used a "statement" pot for this project, which I bought in France many years ago in a pottery. I love its imperfections and colours, and it has become one of my prized possessions. Despite its rustic Provençal origins, it looks elegant in an urban front garden potted up with a three-tier layer of plants that complement the glaze.

The three plants I have included are used sparingly to add rather than draw attention away from the pot. The central showstopper is the dogwood *Cornus sericea* 'Flaviramea', which has eye-catching lime-coloured winter stems. The early flowering narcissus 'Tête-à-Tête' is a dwarf variety – just the right height to add a second layer of interest, with its clusters of deep golden-yellow trumpets that help to bring the scheme alive. Finally, I have created a third layer of underplanting with cushions of yellow-green variegated lemon thyme. The foliage gives off a citrussy aroma when you brush against it and can be used from spring to autumn in the kitchen.

1. Collect together all your plants and assess your pot's suitability. When filled with soil, mine is very heavy and its urn shape is not ideal for shrubs – the roots will fill it out and then be impossible to remove.

2. To protect a terracotta pot from damage, use a light plastic pot with drainage holes in the base that fits snugly inside it. Trim off the rim so it sits just above the lip of the decorative glazed pot.

3. Add a layer of soil-based compost and plant the dogwood in the middle, so the top of the rootball will be at the same depth as it was in its original pot. Push in more compost around the sides.

4. **Plant the narcissi**, adding more compost if needed, so that the top is about 5cm (2in) below the rim. Also allow space for the small thymes around the edges.

5. **Split the thyme** rootballs into two or three and push the plants between the bulbs, so they disguise the space between the two pots. Thyme has a trailing habit and will gradually fill the gaps as it grows.

EXPERT TIP
If the daffodils need support, tie them to the dogwood stems with soft twine. Keep the pot watered, and remove the daffodils after flowering.

WHITE & CREAM

Crystal clear whites and warm creams will brighten up the winter and early spring garden, mirroring the sparkling frost and snow.

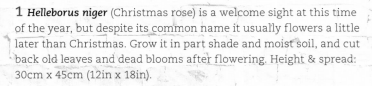

1 *Helleborus niger* (Christmas rose) is a welcome sight at this time of the year, but despite its common name it usually flowers a little later than Christmas. Grow it in part shade and moist soil, and cut back old leaves and dead blooms after flowering. Height & spread: 30cm x 45cm (12in x 18in).

2 *Primula* (primrose and polyanthus) can be bought in winter in trays and planted up in containers for continuous colour from mid-winter to late spring. Choose a spot in dappled shade with moist soil in a bed or border. Height & spread: up to 50cm (20in).

3 & 4 *Galanthus elwesii* **'Marjorie Brown'** and *G. nivalis* **'Angelique'** (snowdrops) can be planted individually in small pots or in clumps in shade and moist soil. Height & spread: 10cm x 5cm (4in x 2in).

5 *Fritillaria meleagris* var. *unicolor* subvar. *alba* (white snake's head fritillary) is the white form of this woodland plant. Plant the bulbs in early autumn in full sun or light shade and moist soil. It also looks pretty in pots. Height & spread: 30cm x 15cm (12in x 6in).

6 *Vinca difformis* (periwinkle) braves the winter in dappled shade, lighting up dark areas with its bluish-white flowers. It is the perfect plant for quick ground cover and its dark green stems spread about generously, even in the dry soil beneath a shrub or tree. Height & spread: 40cm x 1.2m (16in x 4ft).

7 *Narcissus poeticus var. recurvus* (pheasant's eye daffodil) is an elegant white daffodil with a delicious scent, which blooms in spring, taking over from early flowering varieties. Plant the bulbs in autumn in sun or part shade and any reasonable soil. Height & spread: 35cm x 20cm (15in x 8in).

8 *Clematis x cartmanii 'Avalanche'* is covered in small creamy-white flowers from early to late spring. Classified as a climber, the scrambling non-clinging stems of this evergreen will need to be tied onto trellis or wires to cover a wall or fence. It is ideal for a small, sunny or partly shaded sheltered garden where winters are not too harsh. Height & spread: 3m (10ft).

9 *Sarcococca confusa* (sweet box) is an evergreen shrub that produces a profusion of vanilla-scented flowers during the winter months. Plant it near an entranceway to benefit from the glorious fragrance; one sprig will perfume a whole room indoors. Plant it in shade and moist, well-drained soil, and clip it in late spring to keep it in check. Height & spread: 1.5m (5ft).

WINTER WHITES

YOU WILL NEED

- flowering hyacinths
- bubble plastic
- tall zinc bucket
- smaller plastic pot
- multi-purpose compost
- washed gravel
- twigs and moss
- coloured ribbon

This project combines winter-flowering plants in shades of white and cream, blending heights, shapes and textures to create a beautiful temporary display during these cold months.

Grey, white and blue are the colours of winter and the containers and plants I have selected reflect these seasonal hues. The flowers are also among the very first to show their brave heads as winter draws to an end, beckoning in spring.

I have used a variety of galvanised zinc buckets and tins as cache-pots to hide the ugly plastic flower pots. Using the same material throughout coordinates the planting, and I also like the contrast of the metallic finish against this small terrace's blue setting. The city rooftops juxtapose beautifully with the fine details of the planting to create a picture-like vignette or snapshot. I have planted up a hyacinth here but you can use the same technique for the snowdrops and hellebores, using pots in sizes that suit them.

1. Set the ingredients out to ensure you have everything to hand. Stuff the bottom of the tall zinc bucket with some bubble plastic or newspaper. Insert a plastic pot on top and add more plastic if needed so the top aligns with the lip of the bucket.

2. Half fill the plastic pot with some multi-purpose compost. You can mix in a handful of gravel or horticultural grit with the compost to provide plenty of drainage, as hyacinth bulbs dislike sitting in waterlogged soil, especially in winter.

3. Plant the flowering hyacinth bulbs at equal spaces in the pot using your hands rather than a trowel. Cover the roots with more compost but leave the tips of the bulbs sitting just proud of the surface. Take care not to damage the stems.

4. Insert twiggy stems into the soil between the hyacinth stems, ensuring that you avoid the bulbs and roots. These provide a natural setting and can be used to prop up the flowers when their heads become too heavy for the stems and start to droop.

EXPERT TIP
To force hyacinths to flower early, in autumn buy specially prepared bulbs, available from the garden centre. Plant them in pots with the tops of the bulbs just above the soil surface. Cover with black plastic and leave in a cold dark place outside. When shoots appear, bring them inside into a cool bright position to grow on.

5. **Add the final touches** by covering the compost and tops of the bulbs with moss. Then water well. Tie the hyacinth stems onto the twigs with a complementary shade of thin ribbon or twine. After heavy rain, tip the bucket to pour out excess water.

Experimenting with colour **161**

REAPING
YOUR REWARDS

DECORATING YOUR LIVING SPACE

The rewards that come from growing your own flowers are numerous. The more you grow the more you will, quite literally, reap. Whether you sow seeds in pots on a patio or tend a small urban garden, you can extend your enjoyment by bringing blooms, berries and leaves indoors for displays in your home.

With a few home-grown plants you can bring a little of the outside indoors to embellish your living space. You don't need to create huge, extravagant bouquets; I find that single stems poised in tall glass bottles look fantastic, either in groups of different heights or all of the same size lined up with military precision along a shelf, windowsill or mantelpiece.

Start a collection of containers and vessels that match your décor to display your cut flowers and foliage. Personally, I prefer to keep it simple and stick to clear or coloured glass to match the hue of my flowers. I only buy vases when really required, and again I tend to purchase those with simple, elegant outlines. It is useful to have a few of varying shapes and sizes to accommodate different flower groups. A low, squat vase with a rounded bowl or dish shape is ideal for floating flower heads or massing together

an arrangement of short-stemmed blooms; a medium-sized glass cube is incredibly versatile and useful for displaying hand-tied mixed posies; a tallish oval–shaped vase will accommodate just about everything else you wish to display.

Upcycled jars

You can also start accumulating a few jam jars in various sizes. Large types that hold pickles and condiments, especially the catering sizes that you can often pick up for free from cafés and delicatessens, come in pleasing shapes. Or try grouping plain glass cylindrical household jam jars of slightly different heights, and use them to display flowers of the same variety. These everyday containers can look just as stunning as one expensive vase.

Personally, I think that jam jars, hand-crafted glazed clay pots and glass bottles with the odd imperfection suit the relaxed aesthetic of home-grown flowers. The blooms you grow yourself are likely to have the odd twist or quirky stem and will not be as uniformly straight or rigid as shop-bought blooms, so they tend to look more natural if the heights and shapes of your containers are different too. Experiment with the glassware you have at home to see what works for you.

ABOVE **Floating the heads** of home-grown flowers or foraged blooms in a shallow glass bowl makes a simple but effective display for the home.
LEFT **Glass bottles** of different hues are the perfect vessels for showing off single stems. Grouped together on a small table they create a lovely still-life.

Foraged extras

If needs must and I am looking to really bulk out my arrangements, I often turn to foraged extras for a helping hand. Local authorities have their own set of rules and by-laws about what is permissible to pick from common land, so it is advisable to check these before you do so. Generally speaking, however, you will not get into any trouble if you pick sparingly from stems that grow prolifically, but do not uproot the whole plant. For example, in early summer, I often help myself to a few stems of cow parsley (below), which grows in abundance on a nearby area of heath. Likewise, in high summer, the railway sidings at my local station are bursting with the heads of fat purple buddleias jutting out through the railings and practically inviting themselves to come home with me. In early autumn, wild blackberries do the same and, while you may not want to eat them, the fruiting stems look gorgeous in a mixed autumnal arrangement alongside other seasonal blooms, foliage and berries.

Buying flowers for indoor displays

For a special occasion, party or dinner, you may want more flowers than your growing space can provide, or you may wish to only pick sparingly from your precious crop. In these instances, you will need to purchase some extras and, if this is the case, it's worth checking out the flower stall at your local farmers' market or making friends with you nearest independent florist. That way you are more likely to be buying local, seasonal flowers that haven't been flown half way across the world with a stack of air miles behind them. They will also be more complementary to those you have grown yourself. While I can see that the cellophane-wrapped bunches you find in big supermarkets have their place, and that they form part of a global economy, I tend to eschew these in favour of blooms that have been grown with love and care by an artisan flower farmer. Small flower farms are growing in numbers due to increasing demand from discerning buyers, and many offer the chance to pick your own. Check out these independent growers online and visit them if you can. They will also be able to advise you on the best blooms for your displays.

CONDITIONING & CARING FOR CUT FLOWERS

Whether you have grown your own, foraged for flowers, or bought from a local market, your blooms will last longer and look their best if you condition them before putting together a bouquet or indoor display. This only takes a few minutes and is easy to do.

There is nothing complicated about conditioning your flowers. It simply involves stripping the stems to remove all the lower leaves and then cutting them to take off a couple of centimetres (inch) from the bottom, before plunging them into very cold water. This allows the exposed new plant cells to absorb more water and provides your flowers with the best chance of survival in a vase or jam jar. It is useful to have a designated flower bucket or two for this task, ideally one with handles so you can move it around easily when it's full of flowers and water. Keeping a bucket solely for conditioning fresh flowers will also reduce the risk of spreading bacteria to the stems if you rinse it out with a drop of bleach after every use. The bleach will not harm the flowers if any residue is left behind.

Before arranging your flowers, give them a good long drink; submerge the stems up to their necks and set them in a cool place for 24 hours. You can leave cut flowers in cold water for a few days if you refresh it before it becomes stagnant.

FAR LEFT **Buying blooms** from local flower growers is the most environmentally friendly option.
LEFT **Sharp flower snips**, floristry twine and waterproof tape, coloured wires and flower frogs make up the flower enthusiast's essential tool kit. Buy them all online from specialist suppliers.

Fixing blooms into position

Whether you become an expert at making hand-tied bouquets, or if a single stem repeated in a row of glass bottles suits your style better, you may need a little help keeping them in place. Although floral foam is widely used to create static arrangements, particularly for events, I prefer not to use it. Whether it helps flowers last longer is debatable, but because it does not decompose, it is not environmentally friendly.

If you want to keep your flowers in position and prevent them from moving, without making a hand-tied bouquet, try a flower frog or an old-fashioned flower bowl with a fitted lid pierced with holes. Alternatively, use small stones or pebbles or a ball of chicken wire at the bottom of your vase to keep flower stems in place.

You can also make your own framework by fixing strips of clear sticky tape to form a grid pattern across the top of a vase, ensuring the neck is completely dry beforehand. Then simply pop the stems through the holes.

LEFT **Five peonies** divided between a ceramic vase and a glass bottle offers the opportunity to study each of the blooms up close. ABOVE **A porcelain holder** keeps a stem of garden grown geraniums upright. RIGHT **This flower display** formed part of my show garden at RHS Hampton Court Flower Show and lasted a whole week when given fresh water daily.

HAND-TIED GIFTS

Nothing beats a home-grown hand-tied posy presented as a special gift. It is the equivalent of baking a cake for someone and the effort you put in will be greatly appreciated.

Combining a selection of home-grown flowers in hand-made arrangements in recycled jam jars is the prettiest way to present them. Tie a ribbon or piece of natural twine around the jar, together with a brown luggage label bearing a hand-written message, or use the shiny side of a flat leaf as a tag and inscribe it with a gold pen. If it is not practical to transport jars of water, wrap your posy in a square of hessian or a piece of floral fabric and tie with ribbon or string. I keep old bits of material for this purpose, but if you don't have any to hand, a couple of sheets of newspaper or plain brown paper are effective alternatives and also lend a contemporary, urban look.

How to make a round bouquet

Just as you need the right ingredients to bake the perfect cake, there is an ideal mix of plants when it comes to successful flower arrangements. You will need the same amount of foliage material as flowers, or more. Work in uneven numbers of blooms and combine them with a selection of seasonal berries and dried seed heads in autumn or winter to achieve an exuberant "just-picked from the hedgerow" look.

Once you have given your fresh plant ingredients a good long drink, assemble everything in front of you. You will need a length of twine or raffia and strong scissors, or secateurs for woody stems, close to hand.

Ingredients for the bouquet
I have used five stems of ranunculus, three stems of bought spray roses, one single large rose-head, nine stems of dried love-in-a-mist (*Nigella*) seed heads, nine stems of jasmine, and nine stems of mixed foliage from a nearby building site and my garden.

1. Collect together all your plant ingredients (see opposite for a list of those I am using here) and strip the leaves from your flowers and the lower sections of your foliage plants, so that you have bare stems of approximately equal length. Arrange all the flowers and leaves by group on a table in front of you.

2. Take a foliage stem in your left hand if you are right-handed or vice versa if you are left-handed. Add the single rose, or other large flower head, with your right hand at a slight angle; take hold of it with your left and twist clockwise. This will become the centre point of your hand-tied bouquet.

3. Work through each group, selecting one or two stems from each in rotation and twisting in the same direction every time. You are holding the bouquet at the binding point and the looser your grip, the more natural looking it will appear. Aim for an equal distribution of flowers, foliage and seed heads.

4. Keep checking the mix as you go, and fill in any gaps. When you are happy with it, fix your bouquet by tying with twine using a lasoo-style knot. The higher your binding point, the tighter your bouquet will sit, so if you are making an arrangement for yourself, work out which vase or jar you are going to use in advance and judge the size of its neck accordingly. Once your bouquet is firmly tied, recut each stem on a slight diagonal, ensuring they are all the same length.

5. The lower stems should all be clear of foliage and spiral pleasingly to give an attractive appearance in a clear glass vase. Remember, practice makes perfect and it may take a few attempts to get the hang of this technique, but with enough home-grown flowers to spare, you can keep trying until you get it right.

PROLONGING THE VASE LIFE OF YOUR FLOWERS

There are numerous myths and tips on how to increase the life of your cut flowers. The essential advice is to display them in a cool place away from direct sunlight or any other heat source, and to ensure that the water they are plunged into remains clean and crystal clear at all times.

To ensure success, keep your vases and jars sparkling and disinfect them thoroughly after every use. If the glass starts to stain, or becomes watermarked through repeated use, add some handfuls of white rice and top up with vinegar, then swirl the mix against the sides of your vase and the stains should lift off. The beauty of using jam jars is that once they have lost their sheen you can put them in the recycling bin.

Replacing the water daily is the best way of enhancing the lifespan of cut flowers. With an extra large arrangement this is not always practical, so the easiest option is to refresh the whole thing by setting the vase under a running cold tap and leaving the flowers in situ. Other tips include adding one of the following to the water: a drop of bleach; a teaspoon of vinegar and sugar; an aspirin; a drop of lemonade; or even vodka if you can spare it. I have tried all these methods, apart from the vodka, and I can say that all seem to work well, so take your pick.

ABOVE **Keeping vases** and containers scrupulously clean is the key to prolonging the life of cut flowers.
LEFT **Large arrangements** can be more easily refreshed by placing the whole vase under a cold tap and running it until the water pouring out is clear.

These ingredients extend the flowers' lives in the same way as the little packets of flower food that often accompany cellophane-wrapped bouquets sold in supermarkets. Bleach will kill any bacteria lurking in the vase, so that is my personal recommendation, but it is worth experimenting.

After a while in water, soft stems produce a green slime which, if left unchecked, will kill the flowers. To prevent this slime, recut the stems regularly under cold running water. I am also not an advocate of mashing stems before immersing them in water, although some professional flower arrangers swear by this method.

Hot tips for delicate blooms
Searing the stems with a naked flame is another trick I use for poppies and other flowers with very fine flimsy stems, as it seems to keep them more upright. To prevent drooping rose heads, which is caused by an air block in their necks, plunge the stems into boiling water and then immediately into very cold water or even a bucket of ice. This will release the blockage and perk them up.

Ideally, a vase or hand-tied display should last five to seven days, and there is no reason for home-grown flowers to die more quickly than shop-bought if you follow this advice.

DRYING FLOWERS

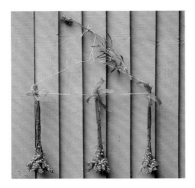

Growing flowers to harvest for drying and preserving, as well as for fresh cut displays, is another reward for your hard work. The following methods guarantee displays that last a lot longer than seven days and provide you with material to work with year-round.

Dried flowers have fallen out of fashion of late, but this can only mean that they are due a comeback. Whatever the latest trends dictate, I like to mix dry with fresh blooms in many of my arrangements. The trick to drying flowers so that they retain their colour is to pick them when they are at their peak. Not all flower varieties are suitable for drying but the obvious candidates are roses, lavenders, mop-head hydrangeas, thistles, alliums, gypsophila, achillea, many herb varieties (*see pp.94–95 for more details*) and most grasses. I especially like to work with the light textured heads of dried greater quaking grass (*Briza maxima*) which is incredibly easy to grow and will dry out on the plant. Quite a few flowers do this to save you a job. Alliums, for example, lose their tiny petals to leave intricate globe-shaped structures that are pure works of art and make beautiful displays. You can even use them as alternatives to gaudy Christmas baubles.

The drying process

Many flowers need some help to dry effectively. One of the easiest ways to do this is to air-dry them. Pick the flowers on a fine day and remove any excess moisture by dabbing them with some absorbent kitchen paper. Remove the lower leaves as you would when preparing fresh flowers and bunch together groups of small blooms or long spikes, such as lavender and gypsophila, and secure with a rubber band. Slip them onto a wire coat hanger so that the flowers are suspended upside down. Large, round-headed blooms should be hung up individually. The aim is to keep the stems straight so they will support the dried heads as they become brittle. Hang your flowers in a dry room where there is not too much direct sunlight, which may bleach them. Most flowers take about four weeks to dry out completely and, although their colours will fade over time, they can last for several years.

Alternative methods

A quicker method of drying your blooms is to cut the stems very short and pop them in the microwave for ten second bursts on a low setting, repeating this until all the moisture has evaporated. Or leave them in the oven on a very low setting and again, keep watching, until you can see that they are fully dried but not so fragile that you won't be able to work with them. Alternatively, if you have an airing cupboard, place some flowers in there and leave them for a few days, or weeks, checking on them regularly.

Lavender will scent your clean laundry at the same time. All these methods are proven to work, but if your flowers turn brown, or worse, go mouldy, it is usually because they were picked at the wrong stage, so do not lose heart and try again.

Choosing blooms

You will come to recognise flowers that are suitable for drying and some will surprise you. I have had huge success with *Persicaria bistorta*; it has retained its pale pink colour really well and looks fabulous with the dried heads of *Sanguisorba tenuifolia* 'Pink Elephant'. Other options include statice (*Limonium*) and strawflowers (*Helichrysum*). Sow seed for the latter in the spring or autumn for a crop of colourful flower heads with papery-thin petals that can be picked when they have dried out on the plants.

OPPOSITE **Dry long, thin flower stems** such as lavender in small groups and hang upside down. RIGHT **The fragile heads** of dried alliums can be kept intact by spraying them gently with hair spray or matt varnish.

PRESERVING PLANTS & FLOWERS

One way of ensuring you have some colour for your arrangements throughout the colder months of the year is to preserve cut flowers and hedgerow clippings. Another easy method to try, the results can be used to make beautiful wreaths and seasonal indoor vase displays.

I love to do this job in autumn when the colours of the leaves are just turning and there are berries and hips in abundance. Preserving is the opposite to drying and rather than removing moisture, it locks it into the plants, thereby prolonging their lives.

Preserving rose hips

A mix of different types of preserved rose hips makes a striking arrangement. Pick them in the autumn when they are firm and a good rich colour. Hips range from bright crimson to a deep, dark black-red. Some of the single roses produce tiny fruits no bigger than a holly berry that look like little jewels, while others are fat and luscious, and almost as large as plums. If you pick them and leave them in water they will wrinkle after a few days and lose their glossy sheen, but if you preserve them, they will last for several months. The technique is very easy, and all you will need, apart from the hips, is some

glycerin, sold by chemist or pharmacy shops as a skincare product. Mix one part glycerin with two parts warm water in a vase or container and stir well. Remove the lower leaves from your rose-hip stems and discard any mottled or brown foliage surrounding the hips. Arrange the stems in the glycerin solution and allow them to drink it up. Leave the stems immersed for a week or so. You do not need to top up the mixture but if the solution turns brown, replace it with a fresh batch. You will end up with a semi-permanent display to combine with dried flowers, or use hips and foliage posies to tie onto seasonal gifts. They can also be added to winter wreaths and table arrangements, and this preserving technique works for other berries and leaves too.

ABOVE **Leave rose hip stems** to soak up a glycerin solution until they have drunk every drop.
RIGHT **If the hips** you want to preserve are on thorny stems, wear gloves to pick and handle them.

How to make a preserved wreath

Either buy or make a wreath base, and collect together a branch of preserved green beech leaves (use the method for hips, opposite) and sprigs of unripe blackberries. These will continue to ripen but to prolong their life set them in cold water first. Choose small apples or crab apples and paint them with a clear coat of matt varnish, and split one large hydrangea head into five florets.

1. Make a base by twisting flexible vine or willow stems and wiring them together to form a circle, as shown.

2. Wire the apples by piercing one side and pushing the wire through to the other side. Twist the wires to secure.

3. Cover the base with the preserved beech leaf stems, using wire to secure them. Wire on groups of hydrangea and blackberry sprigs, spacing them evenly.

4. Space out the apples and wire them on firmly. The wreath will last for many weeks inside or out. When the berries and apples perish, replace with holly.

PRESSING FLOWERS

Pressing your home-grown blooms is a lovely way of keeping a visual record of your garden or outdoor space. Although the colours will eventually fade, keep them in a cool, dry place and they will look good for many years, bringing back memories of their former glory.

I have come back to pressing flowers after a long absence. I find the more flowers I grow, the more I want a long-lasting reminder of their beauty, and sometimes the flowering season is all too short. There are many ideas online and you can also search for instructions on how to make your own flower press or details of where to by one. I have experimented with different pressing techniques but in my experience, using old books as I did as a child delivers perfect results.

Flower choices

Following the same initial steps as you would for drying flowers (see pp.174–175), pick those you intend to press on a clear day and remove any excess moisture by dabbing their heads carefully with a piece of kitchen towel. This will also dislodge any insects. Experiment with as many flower varieties as you can spare and include leaves and grasses, seed heads, slivers of bark, and fruits. You will work out yourself which flowers give the best results although cornflowers (Centaurea cyanus), pincushion flowers (Scabiosa) and love-in-a-mist (Nigella) are all good contenders, as they flatten and maintain their shape well. Very fleshy, dense heads are not so amenable and with a peony or a large rose, for example, you will find it easier to press the petals separately and put them back together to resemble the flower shape when mounting them. Grasses and tiny flowers on thin stems also press well, while fruits and berries, such as rose hips, should be cut in half lengthways to reveal their seed pouches.

Pressing techniques

Once you have dried and inspected your blooms, lay them out and remove any damaged petals or leaves with a pair of small scissors. Place double sheets of newspaper or two pieces of blotting paper spaced at equal intervals between the pages of a heavy book and position your flowers between them. I tend not to mix up the flower varieties because they are easier to label if you keep them separated on different pages. If you have two stems of the same flower it is a nice idea to press the front and the back. The backs of many flowers can be just as beautiful, but we don't often bother to look at them.

Make sure you are happy with the flower presentation as once you close the book there is no going back. Use tweezers, if necessary, to unfurl any leaves that refuse to lie flat. Once you have completed your pressings, the book should

be secured with two elastic bands, one vertically and one horizontally, to keep everything in place. If you have more books or other heavy objects, place them on top or put the book on a bookcase wedged between other weighty tomes.

Drying time will take up to two weeks, and although it is tempting to peek, I have found it better to leave well alone for at least this long, as your specimens will move once you open the book. They will feel papery when completely dry.

Perfect displays

I like to display the best results in clear glass photo frames. You can also make greetings cards and gift tags, fixing your pressings in place with water-soluble glue. Also try wall displays by taping the stems gently to a plain white background, or make a montage on a piece of

OPPOSITE **Pressing flower petals,** heads and leaves in an old book takes me back to my childhood.
ABOVE LEFT **Use pressed flowers and leaves** to make gift tags for personalising your hand-tied posies.
ABOVE RIGHT **Plain metal photograph** frames are the best way to display your flowers and foliage.

stiff card. Keep your pressed flowers in place by stitching them on with a needle and thread or use floristry tape or linen tape, available from craft shops. If you want to keep a journal as a record of your flower growing, then make sure you identify and label your specimens correctly. Along with the Latin and common names, also make a note of any special characteristics and include the date of picking. This will give you something to look back on during the winter when your flowers outside have faded and died.

HARVESTING YOUR OWN SEEDS

The more involved you are in the life of your flowers, the more you come to realise that nature has its own rewards. Although you can search seed catalogues for a range of beautiful blooms, remember that those you have already sown can offer more of their bounty for free.

Although many gardeners diligently order their seeds from catalogues in winter so they arrive in time for sowing in spring, your own little plot will offer up similar rewards for free. Nature's bounty is a no-cost payback but you need to be ready to grab it at just the right moment. This means watching your flowers as they bloom and fade but resisting the temptation to cut them off before the heads turn brown. If you leave them and observe, you will witness the miracle of nature turning flower to seed. Collect the seed heads before they have a chance to disperse naturally or the birds get to them, and you can then sow them where you want them to grow the following year.

Many annual and perennial flower seeds are easy to harvest and some are just as beautiful as the original flower. If you examine the pod of a poppy it is pure perfection, a feat of natural engineering with its own built-in air vents.

Harvesting hints

When harvesting, watching and waiting is key. If you harvest too soon before the seeds are fully developed they will not germinate; too late and nature will have beaten you to it. You will soon be able to tell which seeds are ready and, as with flowers, they are best picked on a fine, dry day.

Using a pair of sharp secateurs, snip off the seed heads and put the whole thing in a paper envelope or bag, or shake it so the seeds fall inside. Label your envelopes or bags straight away so you know what you have collected. Do not seal them, and leave them in a dry place for a few days, during which time the seeds in the pods will probably have dispersed naturally. If they have not, gently break open the pod and release them yourself. Remove the casing and clean off any chaff. Store your seeds in small glass containers, jars or glassine envelopes; then label them and leave somewhere bone dry until spring.

Easy seeds

The flowers that have provided me with the best results are granny's bonnets (*Aquilegia*), poppies, *Nigella*, lupins, and nasturtiums, in that order. All have seed heads that are easy to harvest. You many find that some flowers grown from shop-bought seeds may not look exactly the same, in terms of their colour or shape, as those sown from their harvested seeds, but this is part of the fun.

ABOVE **Harvest and resow seeds** from the dried heads of love-in-a-mist (*Nigella*) by gently breaking the casing and scattering the black pips where they are to grow.

How to make your own seed bombs

You can make your own seed bombs very easily. They offer a good way of mixing different varieties, so that when the seeds germinate you end up with a beautiful group of flowers that look as if they have self-sown naturally.

1. **MIx a handful** of multi-purpose compost with some clay soil, a couple of pinches of harvested or bought seed and a few drops of water.

2. **Your own harvested** seeds are perfect for this project. If you do not have any clay soil in the garden, you can use a little shop-bought clay from a craft store instead. Knead the mix well with your fingers so that you incorporate all the seeds into it.

3. **Divide the mixture** into small amounts and roll these so that each is about the size of a golf ball. Leave the bombs in a cool place to dry out. Then store them in a cool, dry area, such as a shed, until you are ready to sow them in spring.

4. **In early spring,** if sowing hardy seeds, or later for half-hardy types, break up and scatter the bombs on multi-purpose or soil-based compost in pots or window boxes, or over raked soil in a border, away from trees and shrubs. The seeds will start to germinate after it has rained. You can also give the bombs away as gifts: present them in brown paper or coloured tissue, together with a few sowing instructions.

MAKING EDIBLE FLORAL TREATS

As a final reward, many of the flowers featured in this book can be used in the kitchen as well as in floral decorations. I have devised a number of recipes that include scented flower flavourings as an ingredient, and I also use home-grown blooms to dress up cakes.

Real flowers can be used to flavour food, but you are more likely to get a distinct aromatic taste if you use distilled culinary waters and essences. These are generally available in the baking areas of large supermarkets and also in Middle Eastern stores, where rosewater and orange blossom essence, in particular, are used widely in both sweet and savoury dishes. You can also buy flower syrups and cordials or make your own by boiling petals with water and sugar and then straining them well before bottling and sealing. These are perfect for making ice creams and sorbets and adding to cakes, desserts and cocktails.

Crystallising edible blooms

For some extra floral zing, embellish your home baking with freshly picked edible flowers. You can crystallise the petals of roses, violas and pinks by painting them with egg white and dusting them with icing sugar. Leave them to dry overnight before applying another coat or two, and then put them aside to harden. Use them to decorate home-made chocolates, truffles, biscuits, cup cakes, macaroons or meringues. Serve with a flower-flavoured infusion or a sparkling floral cocktail as a toast to celebrate all that is truly wonderful about a flower-filled life.

ABOVE **Serve flower-flavoured** cocktails and iced flower infusions to complement sweet treats.
OPPOSITE **Decorate home-made fairy cakes** and muffins with crystallised petals and whole blooms for an added flower-themed twist.

Simple flower & plant recipes

If you want to eat your home-grown flowers, ensure they are organically grown and not treated with any chemicals, and do not use foraged flowers or florist-bought blooms for cooking.

Flower meringues

Ingredients
- 4 egg whites
- 250g (9oz) caster sugar
- 1 tsp rose essence/syrup
- 2 tsp red food colouring
- crystallised rose petals

Method
- Beat the egg whites until they are stiff. Gradually add the sugar spoon by spoon until the mixture takes on a sheen.
- Fold in the rose essence gently. Add the food colouring and swirl through the mixture.
- Spoon out small portions evenly on parchment paper.
- Bake at 150°C (300°F) for about 1 hour. Leave to cool, then decorate with rose petals.

Flavoured sugar

Ingredients
- 1 tsp previously dried lavender flowers, or 1 tbsp fresh but dry lavender flowers
- 225g (8oz) caster sugar
- airtight spice jar or jam jar

Method
- Add a layer of sugar to the bottom of a jar and then add a layer of lavender flowers. Continue to layer to the top of the jar, seal with a screw lid or cork and give it a good shake.
- The sugar soon takes on a lavender flavour, becoming stronger over time as the flower oils disperse. Keep for 6 months.
- Use it to add flavour to muffin, shortbread or cookie recipes.

Sparkling floral cordial

Ingredients
- 20 scented pink rose heads
- 900g (32oz) granulated sugar
- 2 litres (68 fluid oz) still mineral water
- half a lemon, sliced
- sparkling mineral water
- clean bottles

Method
- Remove the rose petals and put them into a large bowl or pan with the sugar, still mineral water and lemon slices.
- Cover and leave to infuse for 24 hours, stirring occasionally.
- Strain the liquid and decant into clean bottles. Refrigerate and serve diluted with the sparkling water and crushed ice.

USEFUL RESOURCES

For props and containers used in many of the projects in the book, including those on pages 112-3, 116-7, 120-1, and 140-1, visit Urban Flowers: urban-flowers.co.uk

ACCESSORIES, CONTAINERS, VASES & TOOLS
Anthropologie: anthropologie.com
Burgon & Ball: burgonandball.com
Designers Guild: designersguild.com
Garden Trading: gardentrading.co.uk
Nkuku: nkuku.com
Oliver Bonas: oliverbonas.com
Plantation: patanowska.pl
Petersham Nurseries: petershamnurseries.com
RE: re-foundobjects.com
West Elm: westelm.co.uk
Vintage Matters: vintagematters.co.uk

BULBS
Jacques Amand Intl: jacquesamandintl.com
Peter Nyssen: peternyssen.com

CRYSTALLISED FLOWERS
Meadowsweet flowers:
meadowsweetflowers.co.uk

CUT FLOWERS
Columbia Road Market: columbiaroad.info
New Covent Garden Market:
newcoventgardenmarket.com
Windmill Farm Flowers:
windmillfarmflowers.co.uk

DRIED FLOWER HEADS & HERBAL REMEDIES
Neal's Yard Remedies: nealsyardremedies.com

FLORISTRY WIRES, RIBBON & TWINE
C. Best Ltd: cbest.co.uk
MacCulloch & Wallis: macculloch-wallis.co.uk
Nutscene: nutscene.com

FLOWER-FLAVOURED CORDIALS & TEAS
The East India Company: eicfinefoods.com

GRASSES
Knoll Gardens: knollgardens.co.uk

PLANT SEEDS
Floret: floretflowers.com
Higgledy Garden: higgledygarden.com
Thompson & Morgan: thompson-morgan.com
Sarah Raven: sarahraven.com

PLANT SUPPORTS AND TRELLIS
Plant Belles: plantbelles.co.uk

PRESSED FLOWERS
Mr Studio London: mrstudiolondon.co.uk

ROSES
David Austin Roses: davidaustinroses.com

SEDUM MATTING
Green Roofs Direct: greenroofsdirect.com

SEEDLINGS, PLUG PLANTS, BEDDING & PERENNIALS
The Boma: bomagardencentre.co.uk
Clifton Nurseries: cliftonnurseries.co.uk
Crocus: crocus.co.uk
Hardy's: hardys-plants.co.uk
John Cullen Gardens: johncullengardens.com

WINDOW BOXES
Window Flowers: windowflowers.com

INDEX

Page numbers in *italics* indicate a caption to a photograph; page numbers in **bold** indicate boxed text and plant palette profiles.

PICTURE CREDITS

Photography by **JASON INGRAM** except for the images listed below.

NICHOLAS HODGSON PHOTOGRAPHY

All step-by-step images, plus: inside front cover; 10,11,12,13tl & br, 19 all images except tr, 36b, 37bl, 39b, 52, 69tl, 72, 79tr & bl, 85, 86,87, 88tl, 94, 95tl & tr, 96, 100-101, 125r, 145r, 149b, 164,165, 166br, 170, 171, 172, 176t, 177, 179tl, 181.

7, 8 tl **Brian Dunster**; 2-3 **GAP Photos/Jenny Lilly**; 19 cr **Marianne Majerus Garden Images**; 39 **GAP Photos/ Lynn Keddie**; 61 **GAP Photos/Elke Borkowski**; 93 tr **Becky Clarke**; 93 br **Robert Wharton**; 138-139 (Rosa 'Madame Alfred Carrière) courtesy **David Austin Roses**, davidaustinroses.com; 103 **private collection**; **Shutterstock:** 15 br Menno Schaefer; 63t aon168; 64 GoodMood Photo; 76br CatherineL-Prod; 78 Cr3ativ3 Pixel; 91t yoshi0511; 91c sichkarenko.com; 91b torook; 92 Nicolette_Wollentin; 94b Elena Schweitzer; 97t Verena Matthew; 110-111: no.3 Lost Mountain Studio, no.4 Maxena, no. 5 SAMMYONE, no.6 Anna Gratys, no.7 Imladris, no.9 Starover Sibiriak; 114-115: no.2 Paul Nash, no.3 Bildagentur Zoonar GmbH, no.6 shihina, no.7 Ken Easter, no.8 alexpro9500. no.9 photoJS; 118-119: no.4 ksb, no.6 Anna Gratys, no.7 CatherineL-Prod, no.9 Stas Enso, no.10 babetka; 122-123: no.1 Oksana Shufrych, no.2 uladzimir zgurski, no.3 Kevinr4, no.4 tkemot, no.5 Nikolay Kurzenko, no.6 riekephotos; 130-131: no.1 Preeyaporn Suwannarat, no.2 pryzmat, no.3 mr_coffee, no.6 JSOBHATIS168, no.8 Philip Bird LRPS CPAGB; 134-135: no.1 Ruud Morijn Photographer, no.2 guentermanaus, no.3 Bastian Kienitz, no.4 Saruri, no.5 EQRoy, no.6 Alistair Scott, no.7 nishioka1987, no.8 guentermanaus, no.9 kukuruxa; 138-139: no.2 haraldmuc, no.3 Birute Vijeikiene, no.6 joloei, no.7 NokHoOkNoi, no.8 Anna Gratys, no.9 Varts; 142-143: no.1 Tony Baggett, no.5 JRJfin, no.6 jhjunker, no.7 EQRoy, no.8 Katarzyna Mazurowska; 146-147: no.5 mr_coffee, no.6 flowermedia, no.7 mr_coffee, no.9 Landscape Nature Photo, no.10 guentermanaus; 150-151: no.3 choi hyekyung, no.7 Peter Turner Photography, no.9 Yulia-Bogdanova, no.10 Manfred Ruckszio; 154-155: no.6 kay roxby; p166 bottom left Ronald Wilfred Jansen; 176 bottom sunsinger; 178 march.photo

DESIGNERS CREDITS:

2-3 Sarah Keyser for Living Landscapes, The City Twitchers Garden, RHS HCFS 2015; 6 Beautiful Borders Garden Design, New Horizons Garden RHS Hampton Court Flower Show (HCFS) 2016; 9,10,11 Carolyn Dunster; 12bl Dan Pearson Studio;14r Steve Dimmock, The Drought Garden, RHS HCFS 2016; 14l Dan Pearson Studio; 20b Dan Pearson Studio; 21 Dan Pearson Studio; 31 Peter Reader Landscapes; 32br Plant Belles, RHS HCFS 2016; 37 Alitex Garden, RHS HCFS 2016; 39 Teresa Davies, Steve Putnam and Samantha Hawkins; 42 Gary Price, Inner City Grace Garden, RHS HCFS 2016; 53 Jenny and Alex Maddock for Plant Belles RHS HCFS 2016; 55 Emma Griffin Gardens; 63 Peter Reader Landscapes; 65cl, Dan Pearson Studio; 65b Peter Reader Landscapes; 66tl Peter Reader Landscapes; 67b Fisher Tomlin & Bowyer, The Bowel Disease Garden, RHS HCFS 2016; 68 Caledonian Park, London N7; 69tl Great Dixter; 70-71 Carolyn Dunster & Noemi Mercurelli, Katie's Garden – A Cut Flower Garden for Katie's Lymphoedema Fund, RHS HCFS 2016 Winner of People's Choice Award; 77t Dan Pearson Studio; 75bl Emma Griffin Gardens.

AUTHOR'S ACKNOWLEDGEMENTS

I have been writing this book in my head for many years. Enormous thanks go to Andrew Dunn and Helen Griffin at Frances Lincoln Publishers for commissioning me, and to my editor, Zia Allaway, and designer, Becky Clarke, for turning my ideas into a reality. Jason Ingram's beautiful photography has brought my words to life, and I am indebted to him for sharing his talent and expertise with me.

The step by step photographs were taken by my husband, Nick Hodgson. I would like to thank him, not just for his work on this book but for all the support and help that he and our three darling children, Emily, Alice and Edward, have given me since I started my business from home 16 years ago. The late Jane Packer encouraged me to believe that I could make a career out of working with flowers and our kitchen soon turned into a flower shop with buckets of blooms on every surface. My business quickly became another demanding member of the family and the children would often come home to find a vat of melting candle wax simmering on the hob in lieu of supper. They all learnt how to make a hand-tied bouquet while still at primary school and became dab hands at tying the perfect bow. My dearly departed father-in-law, Ivor Hodgson, kindly took on the role of logistics manager and delivery man.

My next door neighbour Eda Longho has given me many seeds and cuttings and shown me that it is entirely possible to create a beautiful flower garden on an inner city street. Claire Sivewright has offered me much advice over the years, while her legal and business acumen has kept me on the right path. Fiona Cartwright generously lent me some of her lovely props, and my daughter Alice, the baker in our family, made the delicious fairy cakes for me to decorate. A thank you also goes to Dan Pearson Studio and Argent LLP for taking time to talk to me about the landscaping at King's Cross. And to Laura Nicolson for proofreading the book and Michele Moody for the index.

Thank you also to everyone who allowed us to photograph their urban spaces: Tom Bannatyne; Fiona Cartwright; Sarah Cusk; Adam Dorrien-Smith at 38 Clifton; Global Generation; Aline Johnson; Jo Lal; Ruth Petrie; Julie Ritter at Floral Angels; Lisa Sewards; Jennifer Tripp-Black; Mary Wiggin at Co-Existence and Sarah Wigglesworth at Sarah Wigglesworth Architects.

Finally, my father, Brian Dunster, and my two sisters, Jo Samuels and Rosalind Dunham, have witnessed at first hand how flowers have shaped my life from an early age. The last year has been very difficult for us all. This book is dedicated to my mother, Sonia Dunster, who taught me to love and cherish the natural world and how to garden and nurture plants, as well as how and when to cut what we grew so that our home was always filled with freshly picked flowers. Her voice is on every page.

Frances Lincoln Limited
74–77 White Lion Street
London N1 9PF

Urban Flowers
Copyright © Frances Lincoln Limited 2017
Text copyright © Carolyn Dunster
Photographs copyright © Jason Ingram
except for those listed on p191
Edited by Zia Allaway
Design by Becky Clarke Design

First Frances Lincoln edition 2017

A catalogue record for this book is available from the British Library.

ISBN 978-0-7112-3862-6

Printed and bound in China

9 8 7 6 5 4 3 2 1

Quarto is the authority on a wide range of topics.

Quarto educates, entertains and enriches the lives of our readers – enthusiasts and lovers of hands-on living.

www.QuartoKnows.com